150 People, Places, and Things You Never Knew Were Catholic

150

People, Places, and Things You Never Knew Were Catholic

JAY COPP

Our Sunday Visitor
Huntington, Indiana

Our Sunday Visitor Publishing Division
Our Sunday Visitor, Inc.
200 Noll Plaza
Huntington, IN 46750
www.osv.com
1-800-348-2440

ISBN: 978-1-68192-754-1 (Inventory No. T2625)
1. RELIGION—Christianity—Catholic.
2. RELIGION—Faith.
3. RELIGION—Inspirational.
eISBN: 978-1-68192-755-8
LCCN: 2022935583

Cover and interior design: Lindsey Riesen
Cover art: Adobe Stock and from interior, see photo credits at back
Interior art: See photo credits at back

PRINTED IN THE UNITED STATES OF AMERICA

*For my mom, Grace, who saw God in an ordinary day
and in ordinary people and lived up to her name*

The fullness of joy is to behold God in everything.
— Julian of Norwich

• • •

*Are not two sparrows sold for a penny? And not one of them
will fall to the ground without your Father's will.*
— Matthew 10:29

• • •

Now there are varieties of gifts, but the same Spirit.
— 1 Corinthians 12:4

CONTENTS

PREFACE

On a given day, you may not go to Mass or pray — but good luck getting through twenty-four hours without experiencing the impact of Catholicism. Woken up by an alarm? Checked the time? The mechanical clock was invented in the tenth century by a monk who became pope. Cornflakes for breakfast? The milk is safe thanks to Louis Pasteur, a devout Catholic whose research was driven by a love of God and humanity.

Running late for work, driving too fast, and heart pounding because of the flashing red light in your mirror? We expect law enforcement to be civil — a far cry from the norm long ago. In the Middle Ages, the law was harsh and unsparing. Fortunately, inspired by the rigor and judiciousness of canon (Church) law, rational regulations supplanted trial by ordeal. So don't fret over a ticket — it's better than being dunked in water.

Perhaps you have a good job because you went to college. The university was a Catholic innovation. Stopping at the hospital after work to visit a sick parent? The Greeks and Romans had some admirable civic virtues, but caring for the ill was not one of them. Early Christians, motivated by love, began the first hospitals.

Relaxing with a beer or a glass of wine once you get home? Monks in the Middle Ages, sequestered in their monasteries and needing to fend for themselves, were the first brewmasters and also significantly advanced the art of winemaking.

Curling up with a good book by a literary giant? Rough-and-tumble Papa Hemingway was a disillusioned member of the Lost Generation, but as a Catholic, he also searched for God as diligently as he hunted big game in Africa. Ending the day in front of the TV with Colbert, Kimmel, or Fallon? If they paused from their wisecracks, the three former altar boys would be glad to tell you that their faith is an essential part of their identity.

There is more — much more. Catholics today put religion in one box and the real, everyday world, especially the realms of science and technology, in another box. That's diametrically opposed to centuries of history. Many of the most important scientists centuries ago were priests. In the Middle Ages and beyond, the Church trumpeted reason and nurtured free inquiry and scholarship at universities. The intellectuals of the those days did not waste their time arguing about how many angels could fit on a pinhead. They had real work to do. Their research and reasoning led to the great discoveries and innovations that ushered in our modern world.

Copernicus, who upended the belief that the earth was the center of the universe, was not scorned or repressed by the Church. Nor did his discoveries shake his faith. Like most Church authorities, he understood that science was a window to the divine. "Who could live in close contact with the most consummate order and divine wisdom and not feel drawn to the loftiest aspirations? Who could not adore the Architect of all these things?" he asked. "How exceedingly fine is the godlike work of the Best and Greatest Artist." True, as everyone knows, Galileo was persecuted. But he was the rare scientist then treated thus. A cardinal who defended Galileo spoke for many Church leaders when he said, "The intention of the Bible is to teach us how to go to heaven, not how the heavens go."

Our technological wonders — our smartphones, computers, and all the rest — are byproducts of science, and science grew within the ample bosom of the Catholic Church. This viewpoint is not parochial, an outgrowth of Catholic pride and boosterism. Historians of science agree that the Church fostered the scientific revolution, unique to Western civilization. Catholicism formed the modern world as we know it, as writer Thomas Woods Jr. convincingly argued in his eye-opening book *How the Catholic Church Built Western Civilization*.

Few Catholics appreciate the role of our faith in undergirding our social, cultural, legal, and educational heritage. Our faith was especially critical to the development of America and its ideals. Americans are quick to cite what formed our nation: the Pilgrims and the pioneers, the Declaration and the Constitution, Washington, Jefferson, and Lincoln. Yes, these people and principles were immeasurably important. But Catholicism was a quiet lever that opened the door to new and better ways of thinking about government and freedoms.

Consider our belief in liberty. The concept of natural rights didn't just pop into the heads of John Locke and others as they wandered past sheep and oxen in the English countryside. Catholics believed that people, as children of God, possessed an inherent dignity. Canon law championed natural rights. Without the Church's promotion of human dignity, it's hard to imagine the Declaration of Independence and the Constitution. God shed his grace on America but not before Catholicism stressed that people are called to serve as co-creators of the kingdom. We cooperate with grace to draw closer to God and to his kingdom. As stewards of creation, we're called to discover, cherish, and profit from divinely ordered nature.

Our enduring customs, pastimes, practices, and institutions can often be traced back to an inventive, resourceful, devout Catholic individual. In the words of Saint Augustine: "God provides the wind; man must raise the sail." In modern times, we're still raising the sail. Our faith guides and informs us. Animated by faith, we discover, explore, build, create, and reveal. We improve society and enrich our culture as we chart our own individual pilgrim's progress, thanks to the power and strength of our fundamental beliefs. We delightfully heed St. Irenaeus: "God's glory is the human creature fully alive."

In the past, progress flowed from the institutional Church, then dominant in society and dictating the terms of engagement with the world. Today, Catholics feel free to spread their wings where they will, while still flying with an internal spiritual radar. We carve out our little space in the world as Catholics, and that space is thus carved up as Catholic. Our work, play, and creativity spring from our faith. "I write the way I do because … I am a Catholic," proclaimed Flannery O'Connor. Faith, even for the famous, gives meaning. "When you align yourself with God's purpose as described in the Scriptures, something special happens to your life," said Bono of U2. "I like being Catholic," Babe Ruth said, "because it's like a batting average. It sets a standard to measure myself."

For centuries, we have read of the outstanding deeds, virtues, and faith of the saints and found those discoveries edifying. Many were priests and nuns (or virgins). The more contemporary Catholics — not all saints — in these pages are writers and singers, husbands and wives, men and women, seemingly cut from the same cloth as you and I. We can be equally, if not more, edified by how they stay tied to their faith and anchor their lives in what they believe, despite maneuvering in decidedly secular environments. As Bruce Springsteen sang very early in his career, "It's hard to be a saint in the city."

It's easy to bemoan the half-filled churches of today, an unfortunately far cry from the bursting pews of the 1950s and 1960s. Still, faith flexes its muscles and rears its beautiful head in recording studios, in locker rooms of professional sports, in the pages of best-selling novels, and on the screens of multiplexes. Catholics are living and expressing their faith seven days of the week.

Sadly, among both Catholics and non-Catholics, Catholicism is often described and demeaned as an instrument of guilt or a repressive force against pleasure. Groucho Marx was once approached by a priest, who thanked him for the happiness he brought to the world. Eying the priest's collar, Groucho said, "Thank you for all the happiness you've taken out of this world." Ouch. And not close to the truth.

According to surveys done by the National Opinion Research Center, Catholics are significantly more likely than Protestants to believe the world is good rather than evil, that art and music teach about God, and that a good person must address the problems of the world. More so than those of other faiths, Catholics affirm life, affirm art and music, and affirm pleasure, wrote the late Fr. Andrew Greeley of the research center. Catholics believe that the sacred is everywhere and walks among us. Everyday pursuits and objects convey God's presence to us and stir our natural impulse to seek the divine in the world. God is not confined to the pages of the Bible. For Catholics, he is immanent, inextricably woven into daily life.

We should not fall prey to disillusionment or discouragement in believing society has lost its way and is frozen in a cold secularism. Every age laments its lost innocence, its failure to measure up to the piety of the past. In the eighteenth century, Jesuit priest Jean-Pierre de Caussade wrote, "Thou speakest to all men in the events which happen to each of them moment to moment. We hear perpetually of the 'early centuries,' 'the times of the saints.' What a way to talk!"

De Caussade understood that God transcends time and place by being present in all times and all places. "Are not all times the successive effects of the divine operation which pours itself forth on all the instants of time, filling them, sanctifying them, supernaturalizing them all?" he wrote. "Everything is a means and an instrument of holiness; everything without any exception."

The divine flows through the ordinary stuff and ordinary moments of life. Even a naturalist such as Thoreau understood that. "God himself culminates in the present moment," he wrote in *Walden*.

God is one of us. The Incarnation binds us irrevocably to him. "Human drives, desires, function and needs are the place of divine revelation and encounter," says Fr. Bryan Massingale, writer and professor. "The early Church authors were convinced that Christ became human so that the human could be the avenue to God."

The Catholic impulse, woven into the hearts of the faithful, directs our thoughts and actions and makes us co-creators of society. Saint Paul exhorted: "Whatever is true, whatever is honorable, whatever is just, whatever is pure, whatever is lovely, whatever is gracious, if there is any excellence, if there is anything worthy of praise, think about these things." Catholics have thought on these things for two thousand years, and the results are manifest in our quotidian lives.

• • •

A few words now as to the inclusion, and exclusion, of people, places, and things in this book. My selections were necessarily subjective,
not scientific. There is no practical standard to measure to what extent a person or thing is Catholic. I have made assumptions time and
again. Bing Crosby not only was a Catholic but also portrayed Catholics (priests, no less) on the big screen. But he's too obvious to include. Likewise for the writer Flannery O'Connor, charismatic figures
such as Joan of Arc and Dorothy Day, cultural hallmarks such as Santa
Claus, or Saint Nicholas, and treasured art such as the Sistine Chapel
and the *Pietà*.

Excluded as well are Catholics such as Madonna, who treats her
faith like a fashion accessory, and the great scientist Marie Curie, who
rejected her faith and became an atheist.

The temptation may be to dismiss some of those profiled here as
"not good Catholics" or to reject them for a known moral defect. Yet
this book is intended not to profile contemporary holy people but, rather, to explore how Catholicism impacts our culture. Indeed, I suspect
few — if any — of the Catholics portrayed in these pages will ever officially be declared saints. Their public lives invite scrutiny and judgment, and inevitably a harsh light is shone on their missteps and mistakes. We have no way, and no desire, to peer too deeply into their lives
to measure their spirituality or judge their moral fitness. On the other
hand, based on the public record, most clearly aspire to do good, to be
holy, even to be saintly, as all Catholics are called to do and be. They are
fighting the good fight.

Some may argue that the Catholicism of Bruce Springsteen and
others included in these pages is known well enough to disqualify them
for inclusion. Yes, the average fan may know that Springsteen is Catholic but most likely is not aware of how central his faith is to his music.
Few profiles of him delve deeply into his profound spirituality, which
animates his songwriting. This is a chance to set the record (pun intended) straight with the Boss and others, to show the spiritual side, or
even the essence, of people and things nominally cloaked in secularity.

Each entry is rich with detail and nuance. Here are Catholic stories full of drama, decisions, and decisiveness that rise above mere recitation of facts. Facts are hollow and one-dimensional, while stories are one plus one equals three. Meanings lie among the assortment of facts. Order emerges from a chaos of details.

Stories are scriptural. God's small voice was in the wind, as the Bible tells us. To hear that voice, you have to be attuned to your surroundings, to the entirety of a landscape or locale. Grace can't be worn and seen like a shirt; instead, it reveals itself in a life well lived or in a book or movie that inspires and uplifts.

Jesus told stories. His parables used common objects such as mustard seeds, vineyards, and shepherds to reveal higher, often hidden truths. Jesus used bread and wine to assure us of his love and presence. I hope that these stories of people, places, and things will likewise offer you the assurance of the overriding presence and love of God.

I

EAT, DRINK, AND
BE CATHOLIC

We are what we eat — and that axiom genuinely applies to Catholics. Much of what we consume at the kitchen table has a Catholic origin, for which we have the monks of the Middle Ages to thank.

You might have learned in high school world history that little reading or writing was done outside monasteries as barbarians roamed the lands. Monks preserved the literacy and learning of Western civilization. Not so well known is the role monks played in protecting and advancing our culinary traditions. The best cooking in Europe was done in monasteries. Monks were experts in farming, a skill that went a long way in the kitchen in an age without supermarkets. The national cuisines that emerged as nation-states developed, even the vaunted French cooking, owe a great deal to the dishes and recipes prepared in monastery kitchens.

Ironically, fast days helped bring about the culinary excellence of monks. Many orders observed more than a hundred fast days each year, but the robust appetites and refined palates of monks still had to be satisfied. Monks elevated meatless cooking into an art form. They also mastered ways to craft superb entrées with humble ingredients.

The literature of the Middle Ages and afterward is filled with portly friars. It certainly was not a sin then to relish a fine meal or a pint of beer, nor is it today. Time and again, Jesus compared the kingdom of heaven to a banquet or a wedding feast. He chose to perform his first miracle at a wedding: he turned water into wine. Who can doubt that he did not enjoy a glass himself? Not only that: Jesus transformed five loaves into enough food to feed a multitude. Ours is a God of abundance.

Our faith also has a sense of humor about food. Saint Lawrence, the patron saint of cooks, was grilled alive.

CHEESE

The history of cheese — which is milk died and gone to heaven, as the advertising slogan goes — is closely tied to monasticism. Cheese-making requires time and patience to experiment with curds and cultures and then a long aging process, and the great monasteries of Europe developed its production into an art.

Munster derives from the Latin word *monasterium*. French Benedictine monks in the Vosges Mountains first made this popular form of cheese in the seventh century, and even today they continue to support their abbey by doing so.

Roquefort cheese originated at another abbey in France. But it might never have become more than a local favorite without an assist from the emperor Charlemagne. The emperor, returning from an arduous journey to Spain and a fierce battle with the Moors in 778, stopped at a monastery near Roquefort. It was a fast day, so the abbey was in short supply of fresh food. The abbot apologized and told the emperor that all they had was fresh cheese made from the milk of ewes.

Charlemagne picked out the dark portions, believing them spoiled. The abbot, with all due respect, told the emperor he was discarding the

best part. So Charlemagne spread the cheese, including the blue-green flecks, on a piece of bread and then quickly asked for more. As he left, he told the abbot to keep him supplied with the cheese. He later rewarded the abbot with a fortune in land and power, facilitating the spread of the now-renowned cream cheese.

Not only did monks create cheese, but the food, in turn, led to the creation of famous abbeys. The Count of Gruyere, knowing the end of his life was fast approaching, resolved to build an abbey as a testament to his faith. So he levied a tax on every cheese wheel in his domain. The magnificent Abbey of Rougement in Switzerland was financed in the eleventh century through the profits made on the famous Gruyere cheese, similar to Swiss cheese but with smaller holes and a sharper flavor.

Yellow, creamy Port Salut cheese was created by Trappist monks driven into exile by the French Revolution. The monks fled to the Swiss Alps, where they had the good fortune to observe the making of several high-quality cheeses. In 1815, after nearly twenty-five years in exile, they were allowed to return to an old priory they renamed the Abbey of Notre-Dame du Port du Salut. They perfected their cheese-making in subsequent years, and by 1878, their namesake cheese, known for its soft texture and robust flavor, was so popular that the monks had to trademark its name to protect it commercially.

Monks were able to develop these and many other cheeses because of their skill in animal husbandry, which left them with plenty of excess milk. They also made good use of their cool stone cellars, ideal for curing and storage.

Biblically speaking, the affinity of monks for cheese is perfectly appropriate. The ancient Israelites were great cheese lovers. As the Bible recounts, David was sent by his father to carry ten cheeses to the captain of the Israelite army. That's how he happened to meet up with the big guy named Goliath.

Pretzels

The pretzel is the oldest authentically Christian Lenten bread. Historians disagree over its exact origin. Around the year 600, monks in Southern France cooked an egg- and butter-free snack they called *bracellae*, Latin for "little arms." About the same time, monks in Northern

Italy came up with the *pretiola*, Latin for "little reward."

The monks in Italy and France saw the pretzel as food for the soul as well as the body. The twisted arms of the pretzel represented a monk folding his arms across his chest in prayer, and the monks churned out the snack to remind people to pray. The three holes in the pretzel? Those represented the Trinity, of course. The monks who baked the first pretzels gave them to students who recited their catechisms without error. From Ash Wednesday to Easter, special vendors once hawked them on the streets. They appear in countless artistic works from the Middle Ages.

COFFEE

The history of coffee in the West is tied up with the history of the Church. Discovered in East Africa around 500, coffee spread to the Middle East, where it became a favorite of the Muslims, who were forbidden by the Koran to imbibe wine. Venetian traders brought coffee to Europe in the early seventeenth century, sparking a coffee craze that eventually spread across the globe. But it is unlikely coffee would have caught on as it did, if not for Pope Clement VIII.

A curious, enterprising Italian scientist had brought the coffee bean back to Rome at the very end of the sixteenth century. Vatican officials quickly advised the pope to ban the bean — a Muslim staple, after all — as a satanic tool. Pope Clement judiciously tried a cup himself. Taken with the flavor, he concluded that something so delicious could not be the work of the devil. (The phrase "sinfully rich" had yet to be coined, apparently.) His papal blessing of the bean spurred coffee's widespread acceptance in Christian countries.

Regarded by some as the apotheosis of coffee, cappuccino has a Catholic origin. *Capuchin* means "hood" in Italian, and Capuchin friars wore long, pointed cowls, or cappuccinos. Espresso coffee topped with steamed milk or cream reminded Italians of the Capuchins dressed in brown and wearing white hoods.

CHOCOLATE

Chocolate was unknown to the West until 1519, when the Spanish explorer Cortés met with Montezuma, the fearsome Aztec emperor. Montezuma was a chocoholic. He consumed each day as many as fifty cups of a dark-brown foamy beverage called *chocolatl*, an extremely bitter concoction of ground cocoa beans mixed with water and fermented corn. The Indians told the incredulous Spaniards that each sip brought wisdom and knowledge.

The Spaniards conquered the Aztecs, but they kept some parts of Aztec culture, such as chocolate. They also had the good sense to make Montezuma's drink more palatable. Around 1550, nuns in a Mexican convent smartly added vanilla and sugar to the traditional recipe to transform the bitter drink from disagreeable to delectable. Back in the Old World, Spanish friars helped popularize the drink as they carried it with them from monastery to monastery.

Imbibing chocolate had been part of the pagan religious rituals of the Aztecs, and, oddly enough, chocolate became entwined in Spanish Catholic religious practice, leading to considerable controversy. Spanish women in Mexico drank *chocolatl* incessantly, even in church. They justified their indulging during Mass by claiming that the drink had medicinal benefits and prevented them from fainting during the long services. The local bishop, outraged at the behavior of the women, banned the drinking of chocolate in church as a blatant violation of fasting regulations.

The controversy was not resolved until Pope Alexander VII weighed in on the matter. In 1662, he famously declared, "*Liquidum non frangit jejunum*": "liquids do not break the fast." The pope probably based his decision on the presumed health benefits of chocolate. No doubt, papal observers of the day snickered that Alexander (much like Clement before him) would not have been so open to the new drink if it had indeed tasted like the medicine it was purported to be.

The Church has a long history of banning certain foods and drinks because of their connection to pagan rituals. Early Catholics were prohibited from eating sausage because it was a staple of the Roman pagan festival Lupercalia. True to the notion that converts are often stricter in observing the Faith than longtime adherents, the promulgator of that ban was none other than Constantine, the Roman emperor whose acceptance of the Faith legalized Christianity and spurred its growth throughout the Roman Empire.

ORANGES, LEMONS, AND LIMES

The missionary priests who made the perilous journey to the New World to spread the Faith also planted seeds that directly affect the diet of Americans today. Franciscan Fr. Junípero Serra, a native of Spain, stood but five feet two inches and suffered from a painful leg malady. Yet, beginning in 1769, he led a band of men who founded twenty-one missions along the coast of California. Serra, the "Apostle of California," carried not only the Faith in his heart but the seeds of orange, lemon, and lime

trees in his satchel for planting in the mission gardens. Nearly four hundred orange trees were planted in 1804 at the grand Mission San Gabriel, near modern Los Angeles. That became the first large citrus orchard in California. The mission also eventually boasted the most important eighteenth-century California vineyard. In the 1790s, it produced fifteen thousand gallons of wine and huge amounts of brandy each year.

Other missions were also the scenes of agricultural innovation and success. Serra's first mission was San Diego de Alcalá. A simple, thatched-roof hut grew into an economic powerhouse with twenty thousand head of sheep and ten thousand head of cattle. Its olive trees formed the mother orchard for the state's olive industry, and its wines won widespread acclaim.

BEER

"Beer is proof that God loves us and wants us to be happy," a popular quote goes. Given that the beer we have today owes its character and quality to the monks of the Middle Ages, beer also may be proof that God is Catholic.

In one form or another, beer has been around for ten thousand years. But monks, ever industrious and innovative, were the first brewmasters. They refined the process to near perfection and institutionalized the use of hops as both a flavoring and a preservative.

The patron saint of brewing is Saint Gall, an Irish monk who got the kegs of Europe rolling when he founded an abbey in the seventh century, near the present-day city of St. Gallen. The abbey was situated near the meeting point of Switzerland, Germany, and Austria, and as an important abbey in the empire of Charlemagne, it had a huge influence in spreading the art of beer making. Today a major brewery, Schützengarten AG, and several other breweries still call St. Gallen home.

Beer was such an important part of the diet in the Middle Ages that it was fondly referred to as "liquid bread." Clean water was hard to come by, and beer was safe to drink since it was boiled during the brewing process. Monasteries, in particular, because they practiced gracious hospitality, needed beer to serve the many pilgrims they hosted.

Europe today is replete with monasteries (as well as some convents) that produce beers to which locals are deeply loyal. Others make beers that are sold internationally. Among the most acclaimed and popular monastery beers are those of the Abbey of Notre-Dame de Scourmont, near Chimay in Belgium. Unlike most, the blue-labeled beer is laid down for two to three years and is often vintage-dated.

Guidebooks on Germany today rave about little-known monastery beers in small, isolated towns. Heavily Catholic Bavaria stands as the world's beer capital, with a third of the world's breweries. Crucifixes overlook the kettles in brewhouses. During village festivals held there in the summer, a priest first gives a blessing in a meadow, and then it's off to the beer tent. Priests and religious are served first — a perk of their vocation.

WINE

Of all foods and drinks, wine has perhaps the deepest and richest association with the Catholic Faith. The collapse of the Roman Empire in the fifth century left Europe in shambles. Vineyard-owning bishops and monasteries carefully protected their vines from barbarian invaders, promoted the spread of vineyards throughout Europe, and advanced the art of winemaking through new techniques that are still in use today. Catholics' attachment to wine even helped stem the tide of Protestantism.

Abbots and bishops owned vineyards in abundance throughout the Middle Ages. They had several advantages over secular vineyard owners. The laws of inheritance often forced secularly owned plots to be subdivided among heirs, making them smaller and less economically feasible. The Crusades and the prospect of death on the battlefield proved to be a boon for Church-owned vineyards. Knights leaving for the Holy Land gave land to the Church in return for prayers. Death from natural causes also benefited monasteries, as aristocrats often bequeathed their valuable plots to the Church.

Monasteries became the place where the art and science of winemaking were perfected, and many of the techniques the monks discovered are still in use today. Monks painstakingly studied grapes and agricultural methods. The Cistercians in particular became expert winemakers; they experimented endlessly with soil preparation, pruning, and grafting, and they confirmed that certain sections of a vineyard produced wines with a distinctive taste.

Monks are also credited with abandoning the practice of storing and aging wine in barrels, as was done until the seventeenth century. A monk whose name is lost to history discovered that a cork helps wine both last longer and improve with aging. A Benedictine monk whose name is definitely not lost to history spent untold hours studying fermentation and bottling techniques before producing a famous bubbly drink that evolved into the world's beverage of celebration. His name: none other than Dom Perignon.

Abbeys became renowned for the quality and quantity of their vineyards. The Abbey of Saint-Germain-des-Prés, near Paris, owned twenty thousand hectares of cultivable land by the ninth century. Some bishops were so devoted to the science of winemaking that they finagled their way into moving to regions more favorable to wine production. Gregory of Langres (who became Saint Gregory) once cleverly relocated to Dijon, the largest town in the legendary Burgundy wine region.

Wine cultivation was almost a sacred duty. The Council of Aachen in 816 decreed that every cathedral should include a group of men who lived under monastic rule, and one of their specific obligations was to plant a vineyard. The Church valued wine, and vineyards that did exceptionally well received special privileges. Pope Alexander III in 1171 exempted the Cistercians from paying the Church tithe and later even went so far as to threaten to excommunicate anyone who opposed the exemption.

The Church required a supply of wine for Communion, so it had a vested interest in seeing the vineyards flourish. Probably more significantly, since few lay Catholics took the chalice, wine was part of the economic infrastructure of the Church. Some churchgoers tithed with barrels of wine, which priests easily could convert to cash. Vast monasteries, compact mini-cities with their own economy and population, relied on their vineyards to sustain themselves.

But beyond dollars and cents, wine was much more than just another form of nourishment — not surprising, considering its sacramental role. Benedictine monks were allowed a daily ration of wine. Some orders permitted monks to have wine with breakfast as well as with supper.

Bishops and priests regularly warned of the sinfulness of excessive drinking, but wine was viewed as a gift from God to be used in moderation. Winegrowers took on a special status as a link to the sacred. They often referenced the first verse of John 15: "I am the true vine, and my Father is the vinedresser."

Winegrowers clung to the Church when Protestantism took root, according to historians of wine. It's not that Protestants wanted to shut down the vineyards, but Catholics were part of a communal faith, whereas Protestants forged a more independent and personal relationship with God. The culture and atmosphere surrounding winemaking were community-oriented. To put it in appropriate terms, Catholics saw themselves as grapes on the same branch, coming together in a union, in the Body of Christ.

So the next time you're enjoying a fine glass of red or white, remember that you never really drink alone. You have the weight of history and tradition at your side.

FRUITCAKE

We have all heard the jokes about the food that seems neither cake nor fruit. "There is only one fruitcake in the entire world, " Johnny Carson cracked, "and people keep passing it around." Another joke: "That fruitcake came over on the Mayflower — yeah, the one you bought."

Not all fruitcakes are made by monks at monasteries, but many are, so fruitcake is a quasi-official Catholic food. As one non-Catholic food blogger wrote, "Catholicism is fruitcake. Protestantism is banana bread." That makes sense. Catholicism is dense, mysterious, and heavy in a way that Protestantism isn't.

Actually, fruitcakes predate Christianity. To sustain their marching troops on long campaigns, the ancient Romans concocted a fruitcake-like energy bar called *satura*, a mix of pomegranate seeds, pine nuts, raisins, barley mash, and honeyed wine.

Christians, of course, appropriated from the Romans what was good and valuable — or, in the case of fruitcake, some might argue, what was not so good. Christian armies during the Crusades relied on a form of fruitcake similar to that of the Romans.

During the late Middle Ages, Europeans came up with their own versions of fruitcake. For Italians, it was *panforte* and *panettone*. Germans enjoyed powdered-sugar-coated *stollen*. The British favored plum pudding, which, despite its name, is actually more of a plum cake.

Fruitcake has been part of Christian England at Christmastime for far longer than it has been popular in the United States. In England, the First Sunday of Advent is known as "Stir-Up Sunday." The plum puddings and fruitcakes that need to ripen for Christmas must be begun on this day. These desserts are appropriate for the sacred day, as their richness and spiciness bring to mind the gifts of the Magi: the gold, frankincense, and myrrh for the Christ Child.

The British delicacy appears in the carol "We Wish You a Merry Christmas." Carolers sing: "Now bring us some figgy pudding." That was a reasonable demand because English nobles in Victorian England fed carolers with a slice of the pudding. That was probably how fruit-cake came to be so intertwined with Christmas, to our eternal dismay — er, delight.

II

GIANTS OF SCIENCE

Barbarians destroyed the Roman Empire by the sixth century. They burned libraries and threatened to erase from history humanity's accumulated knowledge. Monks fled the continent and took Europe's precious writings, keeping alive biblical texts and Greek and Roman classics of learning. Thomas Cahill richly detailed all this in the 1996 bestseller *How the Irish Saved Civilization*.

Besides preserving the past, the Catholic Church played an essential role in ushering in the modern age of science. The Church is commonly regarded as reactionary and dismissive of innovation and progress, with the condemnation of Galileo typically offered as a foolproof argument. Even though the Church, with her theology, philosophy, and laws, ruled Europe in the Middle Ages, scientific progress somehow occurred in spite of the Church — or so many believe.

The truth is far different. The Church was the cradle for the scientific advances of the Western world. She created the university, which nurtured learning and scientific discovery. She championed reason and encouraged scholarship. Catholic theology served as a powerful accelerant to inquiring minds century after century. Influenced by the implications of the Incarnation, the Catholic Church honored the intellect and achievements of humanity and saw science as a mirror that revealed the glory of a loving God.

Non-Christian cultures were burdened by philosophical frameworks that held back science. Buddhists believed nature was impermanent and ultimately an illusion and showed no interest in investigating nature. Muslim scholars made impressive advances in algebra and optics but learned very little about physics and other sciences. They shrugged at those mysteries as belonging to the domain of Allah.

The Church in the Middle Ages saw no inherent conflict between science and religion. Albertus Magnus and Roger Bacon, two of the most eminent scientists of the thirteenth century, when learning began to make its comeback after generations of darkness, were also brilliant theologians. Albert helped shape the mind of Thomas Aquinas, the Church's greatest theologian. Jesuits were leaders in astronomy, solar physics, meteorology, and seismology. One of them discovered the diffraction of light. The list goes on and on.

A skeptic might argue that science emerged from the folds of the Church because nearly everyone in the Western world then was Catholic, and the Church had a stronghold over learning. Precisely — the Church indeed held the keys to the earthly kingdom, and she encouraged scientific discovery, sometimes to her chagrin and sometimes almost in spite of herself. There was nothing to fear in science, as Pope St. John Paul II remarked in recent times. The pope, a champion of science who "pardoned" Galileo, observed that science seeks the truth about material creation and religion seeks the truth about our relationship with God. The two are complementary. "Truth cannot contradict truth," the pontiff concluded.

The First Encyclopedia Author

Even before he died in 1280, Saint Albert was known as Albertus Magnus — that is, Albert the Great. Albert's enormous scholarship spanned physics, logic, biology, metaphysics, the earth sciences, and even psychology. He wrote the first encyclopedia that incorporated the learning of the ancient Greeks. His works compiled the entire body of knowledge at the time.

The son of a wealthy German lord, Albert joined the newly founded Order of Preachers, or Dominicans, in 1223. While at the University of Paris, he set out to make the learning of Aristotle available to Latin readers. Aristotle's books had finally been recovered decades before Albert was born. Albert's thirty-eight-volume scientific opus not only recorded Aristotle's scientific research but also updated and extended it in many places.

Oddly, Albert is most often remembered today simply as St. Thomas Aquinas's teacher. However important that role was, it seriously understates his influence. Albert's scientific advances came at a crucial time in the development of learning in Europe. Scholars had restricted themselves to theology or the liberal arts, such as grammar, logic, and math. Now scholars could access a large body of empirical studies as well as a methodology for doing science. Led by a friar, the scientific revolution was underway.

The Guru of the Scientific Method

Roger Bacon was born two decades after Saint Albert, in 1220. A Franciscan who taught at Oxford, he was the LeBron James to Saint Albert's Michael Jordan. In some ways, he eclipsed Albert, not in summarizing what was known scientifically but in championing the scientific method. He insisted on the utter importance of experience and exper-

iment. In his *Opus Majus*, he set down the guiding principle of the scientific method: "Without experiment, nothing can be adequately known. An argument proves theoretically, but does not give the certitude necessary to remove all doubt. Nor will the mind repose in the clear view of truth unless it finds it by way of experiment."

Bacon dove into his work at the request of Pope Clement IV. Both were distressed at the state of the world, riven by deadly religious conflict. Christians were slaughtering one another. It seemed the last days of the world had arrived. Bacon's urgent mission was to determine what ailed humanity and what could be done about it.

Bacon dolefully concluded that people were too quick to believe what they believed without enough good evidence. He viewed science and its experimental methods as a way to preclude faulty thinking. Truth too often was compromised by uninstructed popular opinion and erroneous custom. Bacon boldly argued that authority needs to give way to experience if the latter contradicts the former. As he saw it, science was a boon to humanity, a literal godsend: it could help spread Christianity, prolong life, and improve health. Bacon praised science as being "most beautiful and most useful."

Bacon was far ahead of his time. Endlessly curious, he proposed flying machines and self-driven boats. Most of all, motivated by his anguish over human suffering, he looms large as the forerunner of the modern scientific method.

COPERNICUS

The Polish genius Copernicus is remembered for his groundbreaking theory that the earth revolves around the sun. His new understanding of the heavens seemed to push humanity from the center of the universe and upend Church teaching. Yet Copernicus was not an atheist or even a deist. He was a loyal son of the Church.

Born in 1473 in Poland, Copernicus studied mathematics and astronomy at Kraków University. He earned a doctorate in canon law (though he was not a priest, as is commonly thought). He practiced medicine and took care of the poor, and because of a treatise he wrote on finance, he oversaw the finances of Prussia.

His day job was as a canon, responsible for a number of administrative duties at the cathedral in Frombork. For relaxation, he enjoyed translating Greek poetry into Latin as well as painting. He was a Renaissance man, prior to the full flowering of the actual Renaissance.

While serving as a canon, alone and quietly, he studied the heavens. This was a century before the invention of the telescope, so he made his observations with his "bare eyeball" while standing in a turret of the church.

His observations led to a theory that shocked the world: the earth rotated on its axis once daily and traveled around the sun yearly. The earth was not the center of the universe.

The popular misunderstanding is that the Church immediately rejected his theory. In fact, several high-ranking cardinals and bishops recommended that he publish his findings. When Copernicus's uncle lectured before Pope Clement VII on the Copernican solar system in 1533, the pope was so enthralled that he rewarded the lecturer with a Greek Bible.

The pope later insisted that Copernicus publish his work, and *De Revolutionibus Orbium Coelestium* (*On the Revolutions of the Heavenly Spheres*) explained the sun-centered world. Dedicated to Pope Paul III, Clement's successor, the printed book reached Copernicus only a few hours before he died in 1543.

Copernicus's finding did draw the bitter ire of poets and Protestants. Protestants eventually came to accept the theory of heliocentricity, while the Church, concerned about Galileo and his belief in the earth's motion, banned Copernicus's book in 1616, a ban not rescinded until 1835.

THE FATHER OF BOTANY

Born in Tuscany in 1524, Andrea Caesalpinus (also known today as Cesalpino) was such a skilled physician that Pope Clement VIII tabbed him as his personal doctor. A professor at the University of Padua, he is regarded as the father of modern botany. In his *De Plantis* in 1583, he meticulously described the 1,520 plants known at the time and classified them into fifteen categories based on their fruits.

Caesalpinus was both a devout Catholic and a proponent of Aristotle, and this drew him into spirited debates with Protestant scientists and thinkers. One adversarial philosopher intentionally butchered his name, repeatedly referring to him not as Cesalpino but as Caesalpino, a reference to the tyrant Julius Caesar. The Catholic scientist took it as a compliment, and the name stuck.

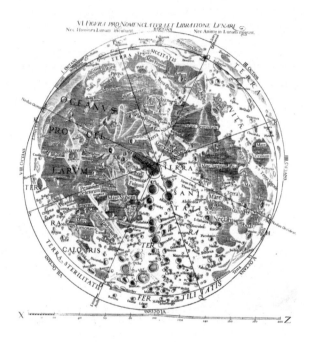

THE FIRST MOON MEN

One of the earliest selonographs (studies of the moon's surface) is *Almagestum Novum*, written in 1651 by Giovanni Battista Riccioli and Francesco Maria Grimaldi, two Jesuit astronomers. Their calculations were so precise that they were able to measure the height of lunar mountains. The book took a decade to produce, and it amounted to an encyclopedia of astronomy. It was so authoritative that scholars used it for three hundred years. Today, Riccioli and Grimaldi's detailed map of the moon graces the entrance of the National Air and Space Museum in Washington, DC.

Grimaldi, who taught at the Jesuit college in Bologna, was also a pioneer for his experiments with light. He discovered the diffraction of light, the slight bending of light as it passes around an object. Thanks to Grimaldi, Isaac Newton was inspired to study optics, and his principle of diffraction led future scientists to posit the wavelike character of light.

A professor of astronomy in Bologna, Riccioli was equally accomplished. He embraced the scientific method with unrelenting vigor and undertook experiments with resolute precision. He was the first to determine the rate of acceleration of a freely falling body. To develop an accurate one-second pendulum, he enlisted the help of nine fellow Jesuits, who counted nearly eighty-seven thousands oscillations in one day. The payoff was stupendous: The reliable pendulum allowed Riccioli to calculate the constant of gravity.

The two priests were men of science, but that did not stop them from casting their findings in a spiritual light. The epigraph for their work on astronomy, insisting on science and not fanciful musings, read: "Neither do men inhabit the moon nor do souls migrate there."

THE FATHER OF FOSSILS

One day in 1666, two fishermen caught a giant shark off the coast of Livorno in Italy. The local duke ordered the men to deliver the find to Niels Stensen, a Danish anatomist working in Florence. That moment is considered the birth of paleontology, the study of fossils.

Steno, as he was known, dissected the shark and was dumbstruck by how much the teeth resembled "tongue stones," triangular pieces of rock that had been known since ancient times. The tongue stones actually were petrified shark teeth, but people then could not fathom that living matter could be turned to stone. Fossils, when stumbled upon, were thought to have somehow fallen from the sky.

Steno investigated and concluded that the tongue stones were shark teeth. He proposed that the corpuscles in the teeth were replaced, little by little, by corpuscles of minerals. He further theorized that all rocks and minerals were originally fluid. They gradually settled out of the ocean and created horizontal layers, with new layers forming on top of older ones — a concept now known as Steno's law of superposition.

Steno further concluded that fossils were snapshots of life throughout Earth's history. He anticipated Darwin by two centuries.

None of these daring scientific theories stifled Steno's faith life. Instead, they propelled him toward theology. Born to a Lutheran family, Steno converted to Catholicism in 1667. Eight years later, on Easter, he was ordained a priest, and he eventually became a bishop.

THE "JESUIT SCIENCE"

Jesuits not only looked up to study the skies; they also peered deep into the earth to discover its secrets. They made so many contributions to the study of earthquakes that seismology has been nicknamed the "Jesuit science."

One of the giants in the field is Giuseppe Mercalli, director of the Vesuvius Observatory from 1911 until his death three years later. To measure earthquakes, he formulated the Mercalli intensity, which is still used in modified form.

Standing on his considerable shoulders was Jesuit seismologist James B. Macelwane, who wrote the first textbook on the field in 1936. He later served as president of the Seismological Society of America. Macelwane's stature in the twentieth century shows that science continues to be an avid second vocation for the clergy and is not confined to history.

Incidentally, the horizontal pendulum used in making seismographs in the nineteenth century was invented by Fr. Lawrence Hengler, a German priest likely motivated to protect his flock. Not so incidentally, by 1924, the Jesuit influence in seismology was reflected in Catholic prayers. The old Roman ritual included a blessing for a seismograph. The prayer included the phrase "for the greater glory of God" — the motto of the Society of Jesus.

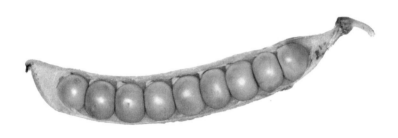

THE FATHER OF GENETICS

Gregor Mendel, a monk in Austria, is hailed as the father of genetics. His painstaking experiments with peas for eight years, beginning in 1854, showed that hereditary traits are passed on through what we know today as genes. His tremendous scientific breakthrough, though hardly known during his relatively short life, puts him on a par with Isaac Newton and other giants of science.

Troubled by serious personal problems and insecurities, Mendel was a most unlikely person to make such an enormous scientific advance. Time and again, he somehow rebounded from a crisis and persisted in his education and search for knowledge.

Mendel was born in Austria in 1822 to a poor rural family. He would most likely have remained in obscurity except for the intervention of an observant local priest. The cleric recognized Mendel's intellectual abilities and persuaded his parents to send him away to school. Mendel went on to study at a university in Brunn, in the Czech Republic, but he struggled to pay for necessities. Triggered perhaps by his abject poverty, he suffered severe depression and twice had to return home.

He appeared once again destined to take over the family farm and lead a quiet life. Instead, Mendel realized God was calling him. He entered an Augustinian monastery, where his troubles continued. As a priest with a duty to visit the sick, he once more became distressed and grew ill. So he tried teaching, but he failed the exam he needed for certification. Not wanting to waste his intelligence, his superiors allowed him to study physics, mathematics, anatomy, and plant physiology at the prestigious University of Vienna.

In 1853, he returned to the monastery in Brunn, where he again failed the teacher exam and suffered another nervous breakdown. Yet he persevered and took a teaching position. The abbot also allowed him to conduct the experiments he wanted to do in the garden.

Scientists then believed that traits of offspring were a diluted blending of traits of parents. Doubting the science, Mendel followed a hunch. He cross-fertilized tens of thousands of pea plants. He used fourteen varieties of peas, which made it easier to control pollination, and chose traits easy to chart, such as height and seed color.

By cross-fertilizing pea plants that had opposite characteristics, Mendel reached two stunning conclusions that upended the science of the day. The so-called law of segregation held that there are dominant and recessive traits. The law of independent assortment established that traits were passed on independent of other traits.

Mendel delivered two lectures on his findings, but his talks were almost completely ignored. Even worse, wrangling with nitpicking civil officials over taxes levied on religious houses sapped his energy and time. He reluctantly abandoned his research, and his failing eyesight precluded him from ever returning to his scientific work. He died in 1884 at age sixty-one, thinking he had failed to make a dent in science. Over the next few decades, however, his work became known and appreciated. Scores of biologists and botanists since have used what became known as Mendel's laws to unlock secret after genetic secret.

LOUIS PASTEUR

We take it for granted that the milk we drink will not kill us by harboring tuberculosis, scarlet fever, or diphtheria. That's because it has been pasteurized — a breakthrough of Louis Pasteur, a devout nineteenth-century French scientist.

Born in 1822, Pasteur was the son of a poor tanner. An average student, he much preferred fishing and sketching over studying. But he stuck with his studies, however reluctantly, and ended up as a chemistry professor. He married Marie Laurent, who became his indispensable scientific assistant.

Before Pasteur, the doctrine of "spontaneous generation" held sway.

People believed that life spontaneously emerged from nonliving matter, and this was why food spoiled and infections developed.

Pasteur's groundbreaking research was prompted by a plea for help from a winemaker, the father of a student of his. Pasteur discovered that fermentation was caused by yeast, not decomposition, and that oxygen decreases fermentation. That led him to realize that microorganisms ruined wine, beer, and milk. He heated the liquids to kill the bacteria, and thus pasteurization was born.

Pasteur's success was due to his scientific diligence. He declared: "Dans les champs de l'observation, le hasard ne favorise que les esprits prepares" (In the field of observation, chance favors only the prepared mind).

His faith also guided him in the research lab. "If by chance you falter on the journey, a hand will be there to support you," he wrote to his sisters. "If that should be wanting, God, who alone would take the hand from you, would accomplish the work."

Pasteurization was far from Pasteur's only contribution to science. He injected chickens with cholera microbes, and those chickens remained healthy when later exposed to cholera. He was thus the first person to use an artificially weakened virus as a vaccine, and he skillfully developed vaccines for rabies and anthrax.

Throughout his life, Pasteur was amazed at the intricacies of microbiology and mystified at the failure of his fellow scientists to recognize the hand of God in creation. He died while holding a rosary and having the story of St. Vincent de Paul read to him, because his fervent desire had been to help children, as the saint had.

He was initially buried at the Cathedral of Notre Dame in Paris and was later interred at the Institut Pasteur. Engraved above his tomb are his own words: "Happy the man who bears within him a divinity, an ideal of beauty and obeys it; and ideal of art, and ideal of science, an ideal of country, and ideal of the virtues of the Gospel."

BIG BANG THEORIST

A priest from Belgium came up with the model for the Big Bang theory, the notion that the universe was created through a cosmic explosion that hurled matter everywhere. Born in 1894, Fr. Georges Lemaître was a professor of astrophysics at the Catholic University of Louvain. In 1927, he published a paper that proposed that the universe began with a super atom that broke apart and formed all the particles in the universe.

His theory was cheered by churchmen, but it provoked a storm of dissent from nonreligious and atheist scientists. Distinguished astronomer Sir Arthur Eddington thundered, "The notion of a beginning is

repugnant to me. I sim-
ply do not believe that the
present order of things
started off with a bang."
Physicist David Bohm
rebuked the adherents of
the priest's theory as "scientists who effectively
turn traitor to science and
discard scientific facts to
reach conclusions that are
convenient to the Catho-
lic Church."

The dissenters had egg on their faces two years later, when astronomer Edwin Hubble made observations from the Mount Wilson Observatory in California that confirmed the priest's theory that the universe
was expanding. Physicists today discount Lemaître's seminal super-at-
om idea, but Hubble had proved him right that the universe had an
abrupt beginning in time.

Lemaître himself did not coin the phrase *Big Bang*. That description, meant pejoratively, was uttered by cosmologist Sir Fred Hoyle, still
unconvinced of the theory in the 1950s. He felt that an explosion leading to the creation of the world was ridiculous, "like a party girl jump-
ing out of a cake." Or, as he dismissively told the BBC, such a start was
a "Big Bang."

Hoyle and other holdouts finally had to accept the validity of the
theory when two scientists in 1965 at Bell Labs in New Jersey acciden-
tally detected a pervasive microwave hiss. That thrumming was not
caused by pigeon droppings on their antenna, as they initially suspected. It turned out to be an echo of the Big Bang.

Even stranger, if you turn on your TV and tune it between stations,
take note of the static. About one-tenth of that black-and-white mish-
mash is caused by photons left over from the beginning of the universe.

Lemaître's thinking put him one giant step ahead of Einstein, at
least on the matter of the origin of the universe. For years, Einstein be-

lieved in a static universe, even though his general theory of relativity suggested otherwise. Einstein could not make "a leap of science" in accepting anything but a static cosmos. Lemaître's theory implied a Creator — Einstein could see no other way around it. Einstein said his eventual acceptance of an expanding universe led him to believe in God. He called his refusal to embrace the idea of a growing universe the "greatest blunder of my life."

III

INVENTIONS, DISCOVERIES, AND INNOVATIONS

Who invented banking (not exactly the most religious undertaking)? That would be the Knights Templar, a Catholic military order founded in Jerusalem in 1118. Dedicated to defending Christian pilgrims who didn't want to carry lots of money and be an easy target for robbers, the Templars devised a solution. Pilgrims left their cash at Temple Church in London, and, thanks to a letter of credit, would withdraw it in Jerusalem. The Knights functioned as the Western Union of the Crusades.

The Middle Ages, especially its earlier centuries, known as the Dark Ages, is commonly regarded as static and devoid of innovation, supposedly nestled in the bubble wrap of the stern and fearful-of-change Church. Think again. Agriculture leaped ahead at that time, through crop rotation and technology such as the horse collar. The economy advanced thanks to new ways to generate power through water and windmills.

The arts, too, progressed impressively. In Italy especially, the Church was the most generous patron of painters, and the Faith was the chief inspiration of artists. Music developed within the walls of churches and monasteries, themselves architectural wonders. A French priest devised modern rhythm way back in the eleventh century, and the history of the composers who wrote for the Church closely mirrors the history of modern music.

So it has gone since the early days of Christianity. The complicated technologies, systems, and organized societal efforts of our ordinary world can often be traced back centuries to a series of advances in science by men of the cloth or devout believers. Additionally, some of our everyday products came directly from priests and monks.

HOSPITALS

Hospitals did not exist in ancient Greece, in the Roman Empire, or on the Indian subcontinent. In some instances, sick or wounded soldiers were cared for systematically; but places where doctors or nurses made diagnoses and provided care were unknown. Church leaders and saints acting on their own established places that took care of the ill, and by the fourth century, nearly every major city in the Roman Empire had a rudimentary hospital.

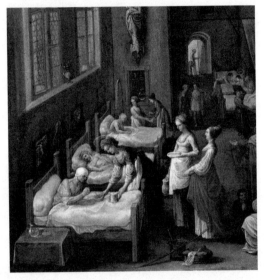

Before Christianity, medical care was often a quid pro quo arrangement. A family tied to another offered what medical services it could. The state did not concern itself with personal illness. "The spirit toward sickness and misfortune was not one of compassion, and the credit of ministering to human suffering on an extended scale belongs to Christianity," wrote medical historian Fielding Garrison.

St. Basil the Great founded what might be the first hospital, in Caesarea, part of ancient Israel. Sometime after AD 370, when he became bishop, Basil built a large complex called the Basiliad, which included a poorhouse, hospice, and hospital. Gregory of Nazianzus, an archbishop and theologian, called it one of the wonders of the world.

A few years later, Saint Fabiola began a makeshift hospital in Rome, and, as a nurse, she treated patients herself. She would even scour the streets of Rome for the poor and the infirm. Fabiola had been born into a patrician Roman family, but after the death of her second husband, she turned her back on her lineage and vowed to live for others as a Christian.

After Rome fell, with the collapse of society and in the absence of other institutions, monasteries provided medical care for hundreds of years. During the Crusades, military orders administered crude hospitals. One military order basically created the hospital we know today. The Knights of Saint John, who were also known as the Hospitallers and were the precursors of the Knights of Malta, opened a hospice in 1080 in Jerusalem for pilgrims. It fed the pilgrims and tended to their maladies.

In 1120, when Raymond du Puy was elected hospital administrator, the Hospitallers dramatically upgraded their medical care. The institution became much less a hospice and much more a hospital. Physicians met with patients twice a day. Strict protocols were carried out, and modest surgeries were performed. Word of this institutionalized form of charity spread throughout Europe, and it was widely imitated.

THE AUTOBIOGRAPHY

The first true autobiography was Saint Augustine's masterpiece, the *Confessions*. Written in Latin between AD 397 and 400, it recounts his wild, sinful youth and his conversion to Christianity. Painfully honest, the work offers an unparalleled psychological analysis of Augustine's actions and motives.

Such a highly personal account was unknown in ancient times. The few other instances of autobiographical literature in antiquity were far less revealing. In the second century B.C., the Chinese historian Sima Qian included only a brief account of himself in the *Shiji* (*Historical Records*). Julius Caesar details his conquest of Gaul and the methods of the Roman army in his *Commentaries* but, surprisingly because of his vainglory, does not say much about Caesar.

Augustine wrote to give glory to God and to help others understand Christianity, but he also produced a compelling narrative of his life and his eventual religious conversion. Later notable autobiographies in the modern sense also found their center in religion while revealing personal details. The best example was written by the fifteenth-century English mystic Margery Kempe. A few years later, after he was elevated to the papacy, Pius II traced his life as he rose from a noble but impoverished family. With the Enlightenment came a flurry of autobiographies, and today we still read the secular accounts of their own lives by Ben Franklin, Jean-Jacques Rousseau, and Edward Gibbon. But it was Augustine who pointed the way more than a millennium before.

Do-Re-Mi

The buoyant Maria von Trapp knew exactly how to teach her unruly brood to sing. Sing along now: "Doe, a deer, a female deer. Ray, a drop of golden sun …" Do-Re-Mi — also known as solfège technique — is the gold standard for naming notes and helping singers quickly learn songs. The trick didn't come out of thin air; as with so many innovations, frustration was the mother of invention, and the frustrated person in this instance was a medieval monk.

Guido d'Arezzo was the choir director at the Benedictine monastery at Pomposa, in present-day Italy, early in the eleventh century. Despite long, grueling rehearsals, his abbey choir struggled to learn the Gregorian chants. The core problem was the lack of an adequate system of music notation. Without music to read, the choristers had to learn the long, complex chants by rote. It was nearly impossible to keep the sophisticated melodies in their heads.

So the monk ingeniously reworked an existing hymn to St. John the Baptist so the phrases of the hymn began on succeeding notes of the scale. The first note was the lowest note of the scale, and the next phrase began one note higher. So his choir learned, "UT queant laxis [initially it was not do-re-mi but ut-re-mi], REsonare fibris, MIra Gestorum, FAmuli turrum, SOLve pollute, LAbii reatum."

It worked. The singers remembered the sounds and quickly mastered new scores.

It helped that the monk had another trick up his sleeve — namely, his hand. He seems to have been the developer of a system of visual signals, known as Guido's hand, to help the singers find the pitches. Holding his palm outward to the choir and pointing to various joints with the forefinger of his other hand, he cleverly signaled the notes of the melody.

So what thanks did Guido get for his startling innovation? His fellow monks were red-hot envious of his success and growing reputation. So he relocated to the monastery at Arezzo, where he devised a second huge advance in music education: the four-lined music staff. Until then, the best music notational system used neumes, small symbols written above the words of songs. A neume indicated whether a melody went up or down, depending on its placement. But how far up or down? If the singer knew the song, the neumes jogged his memory. Otherwise, they were not helpful.

Musicians had tried in vain to improve the system, using different shapes and colors for the neumes. But Guido's improvement proved to be decisive. He drew a staff of four horizontal lines above the text and wrote the neumes on the lines and in the spaces. The result was that choir members could read at sight a melody new to them.

What was the reaction this time? His system quickly spread throughout Europe. In 1027, Pope John XIX invited Guido to Rome to demonstrate the system. The monk handed the pope a book of music. "Please try it," he said to the pope, who then flawlessly sang a song he had never heard before.

THE UNIVERSITY

The Church developed universities in the Middle Ages. These were something utterly new to Europe. Nothing like them had existed in ancient Greece or Rome, despite those civilizations' intellectual prowess and accomplishments.

The start of the university lay in the fall of Rome. The invasion of barbarians and the collapse of normal institutions left it up to monasteries and convents to safeguard learning. Religious orders at first scrupulously and painstakingly copied manuscripts to preserve bodies of knowledge. Over time, they began monastic schools, followed by cathedral schools.

The next iteration of organized, advanced learning was the university. The first universities in Europe were the University of Bologna (founded in 1088), the University of Paris (1150), and the University of Oxford (1167). The curriculum was comprehensive: grammar, rhetoric, and logic, as well as the sciences, such as arithmetic, geometry, music, and astronomy.

These universities were organized in a remarkably familiar way. Their hallmarks were learned faculties, rigorous courses of study, exams, and degrees. Also integral to the medieval universities were well-defined academic programs confined to a fixed number of years and the clear distinction between undergraduate and graduate studies. The university developed over hundreds of years, in fits and starts. But evolve they did, as if there were no other sensible path, to become what we know today.

Given the close ties of universities to religious orders, the predominance of religion, and the pope's authority over Christianity, the pope played a key role in their development. He granted charters to them, in effect accrediting them as we do today. Eighty-one universities were established by the time of the Reformation in the early sixteenth century.

The pope also weighed in on and confirmed the important status of a university degree. This was the age of guilds, and the granting of a degree entitled the recipient to be called master and to become part of the teaching guild. A person with a master's degree could teach anywhere in the world. Pope Gregory IX sanctioned this entitlement in 1233.

The Church not only helped open and grow universities but also regulated them, advancing high-quality education. The Church concerned herself with the standardization of the role and qualifications of faculty, helping accelerate learning and professionalizing it.

The woebegone stereotype of the Middle Ages is that it stifled independent thinking and repressed free inquiry. But almost the opposite was true at universities. There were limits to free expression, of course. But human reason was highly valued, and scholars could explore and discuss scientific, philosophical, and theological concepts. Science began to blossom in the Middle Ages. The Renaissance was not so much a blind leap ahead as a safe leap from the firm foundations laid by universities in medieval times.

Some scholars argue that Christianity alone among the major religions could have created the university. Other religions exalt a divine law, while the Catholic Church emphasizes a divinely revealed Word to be known and loved. Reason was exalted as a tool to understand and unlock the secrets of the material world.

It's no accident that, in the fourteenth century, John Wycliffe, a dissident priest considered a precursor to Protestantism, roundly condemned universities. For him, higher education was a kind of stand-in for the Church. "Universities with their studies, colleges, graduations, and masterships were introduced by vain heathenism," he railed. "They do the Church just as much good as the devil does."

One more feature of medieval universities is strikingly similar to today's universities and, unlike today's universities, is indicative of the importance of the papacy to their survival and smooth functioning. Local townsmen were of two minds about universities. They profited from the money the students brought to their towns, but students were often unruly and nettlesome. And so the town trampled over the gown, as the saying went; villagers and town leaders treated students and professors roughly and overcharged them for food and rent.

In response, the Church flexed her considerable muscles and conferred on students, as potential clerics, the special protections afforded the clergy. It was a serious crime to strike a clergyman, and their cases were heard in ecclesiastical rather than secular courts. Popes often protected scholars in other ways. In 1231, Pope Gregory IX issued a bull on behalf of the University of Paris, giving it the right of self-government, including the right to formulate its own rules regarding courses and studies. Professors could also go on a strike if justified. Other popes intervened when professors were not paid.

Popes acted to put universities in a protected bubble, free to pursue knowledge through debate and inquiry. Promoted and protected by the Church, universities became a haven for knowledge, the primary engine that drove scientific and technological progress. Universities also supplied the growing cities with skilled workers, such as lawyers, physicians, and bureaucrats.

Finally — and for this, they are vastly underappreciated — universities taught, studied, and advanced canon and civil law. Church law was sophisticated, coherent, and rational, and civil law grew from its model. A chief virtue embedded in canon law was the rights of individuals as a consequence of the inherent dignity of people created by God. Ancient Rome and Greece accorded no such esteem to individuals. The often-repugnant moral standards of classic antiquity would not have led to the concept of inalienable rights championed by the American Revolution. It was not a straight line from the medieval university sustained by the Church to modern democracy and the array of individual freedoms enjoyed by Americans and other nations. But our democratic ideals and notions of equality are unlikely to have blossomed without the medieval universities' efforts to develop the rule of law and a codified standard of justice.

THE MECHANICAL CLOCK

The first mechanical clock was invented by a learned Benedictine monk from France who later became pope. Gerbert d'Aurillac ingeniously devised a system of gears run by counterbalanced weights. One of the leading scientists of his day, he networked with other leading scholars in Europe and Spain, which was then under the control of the Arabs and had its own rich body of scientific knowledge. D'Aurillac popularized the use of Arabic numerals and the use of wooden models to study the movements of the stars, and he advanced our knowledge of musical theory and the design of pipe organs.

D'Aurillac became Pope Sylvester II in 999. His tenure in Rome did nothing to dim his intellectual brilliance. A millennium later, in 2003 on the thousandth anniversary of his death, Pope John Paul II lauded him as "the most cultivated man of his time."

EYEGLASSES

Spectacles have a tortured history, at least in the retelling. The invention of eyeglasses is often erroneously credited to Alessandro della Spina, a Dominican friar who lived in Florence in the late thirteenth century. Also often given false credit is his friend, a physicist named Salvino D'Armate. His tombstone in Venice reads: "Here lies Salvino D'Armate of Florence, inventor of spectacles. God pardon him for his sins, A.D. 1317." In fact, Spina deserves credit for promoting the invention. He found out about the new device that made reading, research, and scholarship much easier, and he made sure to tell others.

Well before glasses appeared, the wealthy and the learned used reading stones or magnifiers to help them see small objects. As far back as ancient times, a select few knew that convex glasses magnified im-

ages, but a common device had not been invented to take advantage of this knowledge. In 1268, Roger Bacon observed that letters were enlarged when viewed through a lens of less than half a sphere of glass. He provided Pope Clement IV with a very crude device to help the aging pope read documents.

An actual pair of glasses first surfaced in Pisa around 1286. An unknown artisan had the bright idea to take two primitive convex glass stones and connect them through the ends of their handles with a rivet. The bulky, awkward spectacles were less a product of sheer invention than a brilliant adaptation of an emerging technology, as is the case with many inventions. The development in glassmaking and glassblowing in northern Italy at the time had made eyeglasses possible.

Whoever invented eyeglasses apparently wanted to keep the process a secret and make a fortune off it. Friar Spina and a fellow friar, Giordano da Rivalto, would have none of this. They even preached from the pulpit about the new discovery. A sermon of Giordano in 1306 praises the invention: "It is not yet twenty years since there was found the art of making eyeglasses which make for good vision, one of the best arts and most necessary the world has."

It was Giordano who had coined the word eyeglasses, or *occhiali* in Italian. Spina was even more enthusiastic about glasses, publicizing them and even making them himself. His obituary in 1313 noted that "when somebody else was the first to invent eyeglasses and was unwilling to communicate the invention to others, all by himself he made them and good-naturedly shared them with everybody."

Spina gave a pair to his good friend, the physicist D'Armate, who had injured his eyes while performing light-refraction experiments. That anecdote illustrates how important eyeglasses were: scientists and scholars of brilliant minds but feeble vision now could continue their work even into old age, which is often when a lifetime of intellectual pursuit pays off. The invention of the printing press around 1450 dramatically drove up demand for eyeglasses, and in return, the availability of glasses made books and learning possible for generations to come.

The Catholic connection with glasses does not end with Spina. A 1352 painting of Cardinal Hugh of Saint-Cher shows him wearing spectacles. The cardinal died in 1263, before glasses were invented. The painter likely included them because even at that early juncture, glasses had become a sign of intellectual achievement. Likewise, a 1480 painting of Saint Jerome, who died in AD 420, shows a pair of spectacles. Jerome, who translated the Bible into Latin, is the patron saint of scholars. So today's stereotypical schoolyard put-downs of kids who wear glasses as being eggheads has a long history indeed.

A final association of Catholics with glasses dates from the modern era. In 1953, a convent in northern Germany was being renovated. Found beneath the battered floorboards of the rickety choir stalls at the Kloster Wienhausen was a pair of the early rivet spectacles.

THE CALENDAR

By 1582, the calendar was so out of whack that Easter was gradually becoming a summer feast. The problem was the Julian calendar, which consisted of 365.25 days in a year. The new Gregorian calendar, which calculated 365.2425 days in an average year, set things right. These extremely complicated astronomical and arithmetical calculations were done by the brilliant Jesuit astronomer Christopher Clavius.

CHRISTOPHORVS   CLAVIVS

Clavius was no ordinary genius. He not only translated Euclid but also poked holes in the Greek mathematician's axioms. He was a math pioneer in other ways. Anticipating the decimal point, he used a dot to separate whole numbers from fractions. He used parentheses to express aggregation and used symbols such as the plus and minus signs and the radical sign. These innovations may not seem earthshaking, but the mathematical concepts further opened the door to the technological wonders we enjoy today.

Clavius taught at the Roman College for forty-five years, and Galileo was his friend and apt student. Clavius needled the young scholar about his theories, and it's believed that the brilliant scientist lapped up much of his teachings from Clavius and the eight other Jesuits at the Roman College.

For hundreds of years, Church leaders knew Easter was being celebrated on the wrong day, so Pope Gregory XIII asked Clavius to fix the calendar once and for all. To do so, Clavius had to calculate the time of the vernal equinox. Despite his learning, mathematics then remained rudimentary. It took Clavius eight hundred pages to explain and justify his results. But he determined the correct date for Easter and realized that ninety-seven days had to be added to the calendar every four hundred years to keep the calendar correct. (As brilliant as he was, the notion of "leap days" did not occur to him.) And, Clavius noted, don't forget to add an extra full day in the year 4317 to keep the calendar correct.

Modern Bookkeeping

Ever balanced a checkbook? Or shopped at a business that uses the standard accounting system of debits and credits? You surely have, and you owe a debt to fifteenth-century Franciscan friar Luca Bartolomeo de Pacioli, "the Father of Accounting."

Pacioli might have been known to us even without his bookkeeping prowess. He taught mathematics to Leonardo da Vinci, becoming good friends with the artist and eventually living with him in Milan. He described da Vinci as "the excellent painter, architect and musician, a man gifted with all the virtues." An expert in geometry, Pacioli is believed to have helped the artist work out some of the details of the *Last Supper* painting.

In 1494, Pacioli wrote *Summa de arithmetica, geometria, proportioni et proportionalita*, a brilliant synthesis of the mathematical knowledge of his time. The book also contained the first published description of the reliable method of keeping accounts that Venetian merchants used during the Italian Renaissance. Pacioli thus codified, though he did not invent, the dual-entry bookkeeping system.

His ledger had accounts for assets (including receivables and inventories), liabilities, capital, income, and expenses. The essentials of double-entry accounting have, for the most part, remained unchanged for more than five hundred years.

Besides having a first-rate mathematical mind, the friar also displayed the kind of dry humor that accountants are known for. He warned that a person should not go to sleep at night until the debits exactly equaled the credits. Getting the numbers right was a moral imperative for him: "You will have to look for [your mistakes] with the industry and intelligence God gave you."

THE FATHER OF AERONAUTICS

In 1670, erudite Italian Jesuit Francesco Lana de Terzi published *Prodromo all'arte maestra*. It was a big deal, or at least it became one for the Wrights at Kitty Hawk in 1903. The dense tome was the "first publication to establish a theory of aerial navigation verified by mathematical accuracy and clearness of perception," according to an aviation historian. In short, Terzi is hailed as the Father of Aeronautics.

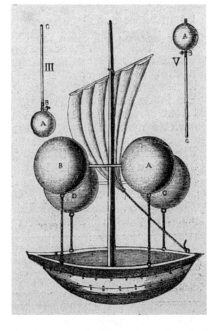

He devised an aerial ship that used a recently invented vacuum pump and the experiments of other scientists. His crude ship consisted of four twenty-five-foot spheres of thin sheet copper bound together. The apparatus would be able to support a cramped basket for riders and a sail and rudder for steering.

His aerial invention was purely theoretical. The Jesuit decided against trying to build and fly it, for two reasons. His vow of poverty precluded him from amassing the hundred ducats (fifteen thousand dollars today) needed to construct it. His second reason was both moral and farsighted, as visionary as his scientific thinking. "No city would be proof against the surprise. ... Iron weights, fireballs and bombs could be hurled from a great height."

SIGN LANGUAGE

A French priest is credited as the inventor of sign language. Visiting a poor neighborhood in Paris around 1770 to offer assistance, Abbé Charles-Michel de l'Épée entered a home where two deaf children lived. Their mother pleaded with him to educate her daughters in religion. The kind priest vowed to dedicate his life to educating the deaf, and in 1771, he founded the first free public school for the deaf.

Deaf children came from throughout France to attend the school and brought with them the signs they had used at home. The priest learned these different signs and helped devise a standard sign language that spread across Europe.

Abbé de l'Épée was not the first priest to help educate the deaf by refining and systemizing a nonvocal language that people had improvised. A Spanish priest, Juan Pablo Bonet, published the first book on deaf education in 1620 in Madrid. His book contained the first-known manual alphabet system. The handshapes in his system represented different speech sounds.

Early man probably used gestures before spoken language. Sign language was part of being human. The two kind priests leveraged skills people had. That is the deeper story here: Religious people, dedicated to helping those with a terrible disadvantage, used their talents and time to bring out each individual's full humanity and to allow him or her to engage more fully with family, friends, and society.

THE FAX MACHINE

The first commercial fax system was invented by an eccentric Italian priest named Giovanni Caselli. Born in 1815 in Siena, Caselli was an inveterate tinkerer. His living quarters as a priest were strewn with bric-a-brac that might be useful in his wide-ranging experiments. In 1857, he began working on a facsimile machine. The first fax machine had been patented in 1843, but that device was so clunky and unreliable that it was not commercially feasible.

Caselli was determined to succeed. The telephone had yet to be invented, and the telegraph often led to miscommunication, so a fax machine would significantly improve communication over long distance. Caselli published his concepts on perfecting the fax machine in a scientific journal he had founded. The scientific community scoffed at his notions and claimed that sending pictures over telegraph wires was impossible.

After six years of collaborating with Frenchman Gustave Froment, one of the world's leading builders of scientific equipment, Caselli hit pay dirt. His fax machine stood more than six feet tall and consisted of a wild mix of pendulums, batteries, and wires.

But it worked beautifully. The "telegraphic apparatus," as it was called in its U.S. patent in 1863, could transmit clear images as well as numbers and letters.

Caselli had vastly improved upon the original fax machine by installing a clock on the transmitting end that synchronized the pendulums on each end of the transmission. Messages sent through his machine could be reproduced in the same size as the original or even reduced. More than one message could be sent simultaneously through a single wire. Caselli had dramatically transformed the first crude fax machine into a workable product.

The French government embraced the new machine and paid for a line to be set up between Paris and Lyons in 1865. The pantelegraph, as it was known, could send 110 messages an hour. Newspapers carried stories heralding the invention. The fax line became a preferred method of quickly conveying stock market updates.

But the machine never quite caught on commercially. The business community didn't want to pay for it. The French government, preoccupied in 1870 by a war in which Paris was besieged, didn't renew the contract. A few years later, Alexander Graham Bell discovered a completely new way to communicate over long distances, and decades later, modern faxes that used light beams to send and receive replaced Padre Caselli's pendulums.

IV

CATHOLIC LINGO

George Bernard Shaw once cracked that England and America were "two countries separated by a common language." The two nations use different words for the same common objects. Americans order French fries, while Brits munch on chips. We stand in line when on vacation; they queue up on holiday. We change the diaper on the baby, whom we proudly push in a baby carriage. They change the soiled nappy and gently place the baby in a pram.

Regionally, Americans, of course, also speak differently, using strong accents that mangle and distort words. In Chicago, my hometown, the most distinctive alteration revolves around the *d* sound. We root for "da Bears," as fans of *Saturday Night Live* know.

Besides place, religion also influences how we speak and what we say. Catholics reflexively use certain phrases rooted in religious belief and practice. "Offer it up." "Mea culpa." "She has the patience of a saint."

Almost without realizing it, we indulge in Catholic jargon.

So does everyone else. Catholics have shaped and shaded language. For two thousand years, Christendom has stretched across the globe, and it has also wrapped itself around our language. Many of our common expressions have a Catholic origin.

BLESS YOU

In the Middle Ages, before science, technology, and consumerism reshaped everyday life, ordinary life was imbued with a heightened sense of the sacred. Ordinary acts took on a spiritual dimension. The devil was poised to steal your soul if you let your guard down. Sneezing was believed to expel a person's soul or at least make one more vulnerable to evil, so people close at hand would "bless" the sneezer as a precaution. The bubonic plague, which wiped out millions, also may have contributed to the popularity of "Bless you!" The fear was that the plague could be caught through a sneeze, so the utterance was more than warranted.

DEVIL'S ADVOCATE

The process of canonization includes a rigorous vetting of the proposed saint. The Vatican appointed an *advocatus diaboli*, or devil's advocate, to argue against the candidate's cause. The phrase took root in the popular imagination as someone who deliberately takes a contrary position in an argument.

HOLY GRAIL

"Holy Grail" refers to a goal or achievement that is both difficult to attain and much desired. The original Holy Grail was the cup or dish Christ used at the Last Supper. According to legend, Joseph of Arimathea later used the cup to catch Christ's blood at the crucifixion. The cup reputedly was later carried to England, where it became a quest of King Arthur and his Knights of the Round Table.

The linguistic roots of *grail* suggest that it could be either a cup or a dish. *Greal* is "cup" in old English, and *graal* means the same in old French. On the other hand, *gradalis* means "dish" or "platter" in medieval Latin. No one has found the Holy Grail, so perhaps part of the problem in tracking it down is not knowing whether it's a cup or a dish.

HOLY MACKEREL

Your mother probably never reprimanded you for using the expression "holy mackerel," but she might have if she knew its origin. "Holy mackerel" is a blasphemous oath, probably a softer, more acceptable version of angrily invoking Holy Mary or the Holy Mother of God.

For many years, mackerel was the popular fish of choice for Catholics on a limited budget, so the phrase is also a slam of sorts against blue-collar Catholics.

Other religious traditions and rituals have their own versions of "holy mackerel." "Holy cow" cycles back to Hindus.

HOLY SMOKE

Maybe the quaint phrase "holy smoke" is passé, a favorite of innocent fictional characters such as Frank and Joe Hardy. Consider it a pious Catholic's version of swearing. Its origins are unclear: It stems either from incense or from the use of smoke in the election of a pope.

KNOCK ON WOOD

Catholics are people of the Cross, the most powerful symbol of God's love for us. "Knock on wood" invokes the power of the Cross when facing trouble or danger. In ancient times, Catholics would knock three times, one for each person of the Trinity.

LIMBO

Most Catholics presume that limbo no longer exists. (And you may have heard the inevitable wisecrack, "So where did it go?") Limbo was believed to be the place between heaven and hell. It was the destination of unbaptized babies, a theologically logical concept. The Latin *limbus* means "the edge." The dictionary

definition of *limbo* is "an intermediate or transitional place." The popular connotation, closer in meaning to its religious association, is being caught in an uncertain situation. The word also derives its popular meaning from the Caribbean dance, in which a dancer is caught for a moment beneath the bar.

NEITHER RHYME NOR REASON

"Neither rhyme nor reason" refers to a plan that does not make sense. St. Thomas More is credited with its origin. He advised an author to turn his subpar manuscript into rhyme. The author complied. More was pleased with the result: "'Tis rhyme now, but before it was neither rhyme nor reason."

NICHE

A niche is a place or an activity for which a person or thing is best suited. That meaning derives from the niches or small alcoves in a building in Paris called the Pantheon, a church that was later secularized. It was used in the eighteenth century to hold the remains of famous Frenchmen. The alcoves held monuments attesting to their accomplishments. The French began referring to "a niche in the temple of fame."

PLACEBO

We understand today that a placebo, used in clinical trials to test the effectiveness of treatments, is a fake drug that users believe is the real thing. But for centuries, the term was understood strictly in a religious context, first in a favorable sense and then in an unfavorable way.

In Psalm 116, in early Latin translations of the Hebrew Bible, the phrase *Placebo Domine* meant, "I will please the Lord." Centuries later, in the medieval times, the Vespers for the Dead used Psalm 116, so *placebo* came to mean that funeral rite of the Church. By the thirteenth century, the term had taken on a disparaging, secular meaning: mourners who were paid to attend a funeral to flatter the dead were said to "sing placebos" of false and easy praise. In *The Canterbury Tales* in the fourteenth century, Chaucer named his obsequious courtier Placebo.

Placebo became associated with medical treatment, thanks to the wide influence of William Cullen, the leading British physician of the eighteenth century. In his famous lectures at the University of Edinburgh, he explained how he dealt with difficult patients who insisted on some form of treatment even though Cullen knew he could not help them. He gave them harmless but ineffective mustard-powder treatments. Knowing the history of the word, he chose to call the treatments "placebos."

QUARANTINE

When the coronavirus spread in 2020, we fully realized, to our regret and sadness, the meaning of the word *quarantine*. The term goes back to the Middle Ages. Back then, as hard as it may be to believe, a person was even less enthusiastic about being in quarantine. It didn't mean isolation (far from it): It called you out for being a flagrant sinner.

During Lent, beginning on Ash Wednesday, people who had committed notorious sins were required by the Church to do public penance. You could not bathe, shave, wear shoes, talk to others, sleep on a mattress, or stay with your family. Nor could you receive the sacraments. The ban on these things ended on Holy Thursday, when the bishop would formally absolve you of your sins. This period of exclusion, lasting about forty days, was called "quarantine" from the Latin word for "forty."

The Black Death changed the word's meaning. When the bubonic plague hit Venice in the mid-fourteenth century, ships arriving from infected ports were required to sit at anchor for forty days. *Quarantine* took on its current meaning of isolation because of illness.

RED SKY AT NIGHT, SAILOR'S DELIGHT / RED SKY IN THE MORNING, SAILOR'S WARNING

The expression "Red sky at night, sailor's delight / Red sky in the morning, sailor's warning" goes back two thousand years, to the Gospel of Matthew. When the Pharisees impetuously asked Jesus for a sign from heaven, he responded, "When it is evening, you say, 'It will be fair weather, for the sky is red.' And in the morning, 'It will be stormy to-day, for the sky is red and threatening.' You know how to interpret the appearance of the sky, but you cannot interpret the signs of the times" (Mt 16:2–3). Jesus was speaking in allegorical terms, but the expression may have caught on because it is, in fact, meteorologically accurate. Another version of the saying substitutes *shepherds* for *sailors*, as shepherds are also much concerned about the weather.

ROB PETER TO PAY PAUL

Who hasn't used the expression "Rob Peter to pay Paul" in exasperation? Well, before the Reformation in England, Catholics there said this with a bit of a wink. They withheld a contribution to St. Peter's in Rome to contribute to St. Paul's in London instead.

V

AMERICA

Since the earliest days of colonial America, Catholics were outsiders, unwelcome, often vilified, and sometimes persecuted. The first line of "Of Plymouth Plantation," written by William Bradford, who arrived on the *Mayflower* and served as governor of the Plymouth settlement, refers to "the gross darkness of popery which had covered and overspread the Christian world." Anti-Catholicism only increased as the population grew. Nearly all the colonies quickly passed laws restricting the practices of the Catholic Faith.

This prejudice against Catholics proved to be lasting. In the nineteenth century, anti-Catholic mobs tormented immigrants, and presidential candidates demonized Catholics. During the 1884 presidential campaign, Republican officials denounced Democrats for championing "rum, Romanism, and rebellion." Al Smith, a Catholic, lost the 1928 presidential election after he was accused of "taking orders from the pope." John Kennedy had to overcome similar fears to narrowly win the 1960 election.

Despite distrust and hostility, Catholics played a key role in our nation's founding, and some of our most cherished traditions and cultural treasures have Catholic roots. WASPs stood astride America with their economic and political clout, yet on the edges and corners of society, Catholics made their mark, eventually burrowing inside the walls of the castle and achieving, in many instances, a kind of cultural coup d'état.

COLUMBUS

A native of Genoa, Italy, Christopher Columbus sailed to discover a westerly route to the Far East that could enrich Spain. But as a staunch Catholic who prayed regularly and was deeply devoted to Mary, he also strove to spread Christianity to the New World. At the tops of his letters and other documents he routinely wrote, "Jesus and Mary, be with us on the way." In his diary, he wrote of the people he encountered in the New World, "I believe that they would easily be made Christians, for it seemed to me that they had no religion of their own."

Columbus was terribly mistaken. Indoctrination of the Faith was, in many cases, cruelly forced on the indigenous peoples. We see Columbus, once an unblemished hero, in a new light today.

But let's go back to October 11, 1492. It had been a rough, dangerous voyage. That morning, as usual, the crew prayed the Our Father and the Hail Mary. In the evening, the crew assembled to pray and sing the Salve Regina, the evening hymn to Mary. Columbus, believing land was near, urged his crew to keep a close watch. Early the next morning, a sailor aboard the *Pinta* shouted, "Land!" The ship was four hundred miles east of the Florida Keys in the present-day Bahamas. The small dot in the ocean is now known as Watling Island, though Columbus named it San Salvador (Holy Savior). That morning, the crews' prayers were said with more gusto.

America is a work in progress. Columbus certainly made the first egregious mistakes of many to follow by explorers and settlers. But the Faith made landfall along with him and his crew, allowing for all else that followed.

THANKSGIVING

We all know the story of the first Thanksgiving in 1621 and how Native Americans helped the Pilgrims grow food. Well, as Paul Harvey would say, here's the rest of the story — a Catholic Native American made it all possible. Considering what he knew of the white settlers and how he had been treated by them up to that time, it was something of a miracle.

In 1614, Captain John Smith (of Pocahontas fame) led two British ships to Maine. One of his lieutenants sailed one of the ships to Cape Cod, where the British explorers encountered a tribe of Native Americans. He invited two dozen of them, curious about these strange seafarers, to the ship, where they were forced into irons and taken as slaves back across the Atlantic to the island of Málaga, near Spain. One of them was a man named Squanto.

Spain was a Catholic nation, and Pope Paul III, in 1537, had issued a bull that forbade the enslavement of the indigenous peoples of the Americas. The Native Americans, he ruled, were rational human beings who had the right to freedom, even if they were heathen. So, before Squanto could be sold in chains, Franciscan friars released him and diligently taught him the Catholic Faith. Squanto wanted to return home, but the friars instead were able to send him to London as a free man. There he learned English and finally secured a passage back to the Americas in 1619.

Squanto made his way to Plymouth Rock, but his tribe was gone — wiped out by the diseases transmitted by the white settlers. He was taken captive by a chief named Massasoit, whose own powerful Wampanoag tribe also had been greatly reduced by disease.

Massasoit had to decide what to do about the white settlers who had arrived, the Pilgrims. He was not sure he could trust them. They had stolen ten bushels of maize. Their thievery helped keep them alive that first winter. Little had gone right for them since they sailed from England, and half the 102 people aboard the *Mayflower* were dead by the end of that first winter.

Massasoit probably could have easily killed the settlers. But he had his own rivals to deal with, and the Pilgrims had cannons and guns, weapons that might make his rivals hesitate to attack him. So he sent Squanto as an emissary to them. The Pilgrims were astounded at his ability to speak English.

The Catholic Squanto taught the Pilgrims how to plant the native corn and how to fish, and he saved their lives in another way. In serving as an emissary and interpreter, he almost certainly turned Massasoit away from an attack.

The great irony is that the Pilgrims were hostile to Catholics and religious freedom. They left England to establish a settlement free of other forms of Christianity. G. K. Chesterton once cracked that England ought to celebrate Thanksgiving in gratitude that the intolerant Pilgrims left England.

Sadly, Squanto did not live long after his memorable kindness to the Pilgrims; he succumbed to a European-brought disease in 1622. His last words, according to William Bradford, governor of the Plymouth colony, were to pray for him "that he might go to the Englishmen's God in heaven."

Squanto, tricked and kidnapped as a slave by white settlers, still treated the Pilgrims as friends. We equate Thanksgiving with gratitude for blessings, of course, but Squanto, in exemplifying forgiveness and charity, helped bring to the New World, to the often narrow-minded, pinch-faced Pilgrims, the ethic of love at the heart of Christianity. Call it the first instance of reverse evangelization.

FREEDOM OF RELIGION

Catholics advocated for religious freedom in the colonies. Chief among those Catholics was George Calvert, who served as secretary of state under James I in England. After Calvert converted to Catholicism, he had to resign, as Catholics were not permitted to serve in high offices in England. Charles I, the son and successor of James I, granted Calvert land in the New World. Calvert died in 1632 before the land was chartered, but his son Cecil took over. The land was named Maryland, officially in honor of Queen Maria, Charles' wife, but some scholars believe the name was chosen to honor the Blessed Mother.

Mindful of the entrenched religious intolerance in England, Maryland established freedom of religion within the colony, a seminal moment in American history. The Calverts envisioned an America in which Catholics and Protestants could coexist peacefully and on equal terms, an ideal that would not be realized for many years.

CHARLES CARROLL

Maryland was a glorious exception among the original thirteen colonies. Generally excluded from influence and power, Catholics faced myriad legal, social, and religious barriers. To be a person of influence and power in the early days of America required you to be white, Protestant, and a man. (Sound familiar?) As the colonies grew increasingly dissatisfied with British rule, and as support for independence grew, Catholics continued to be kept on the sidelines and marginalized. Fifty-six men signed the Declaration of Independence; only one was Catholic: Charles Carroll.

Carroll, an extremely wealthy Maryland landowner, was one of the richest men in the colonies, if not the richest. Even so, Protestants had regularly challenged his patriotism, questioning whether his ultimate loyalty was to Rome. Like the other signers, his backing of American independence put his life and wealth at risk. Carroll risked as much as, if not more than, any other signer. When John Hancock asked

Carroll if indeed he would sign the Declaration, he replied, "Most willingly." A bystander blithely remarked, "There go a few millions."

Incidentally, Carroll's cousin John served as the nation's first bishop in Baltimore. Sensitive to Americans' suspicions about Catholics, he asked Rome in 1787 to allow U.S. Catholics to celebrate Mass in English. Not quite ready for Vatican II, the pope refused the unusual request.

Charles Carroll served as a U.S. senator after the Revolution. President Washington, a close friend and ally of Carroll, asked him to support a foreign service appropriation, the first time a president ever overtly attempted to influence legislation. Carroll adroitly persuaded the House of Representatives to reverse its opposition to the appropriation.

Carroll enjoyed a long and distinguished public career. Besides serving as a senator, he helped develop Maryland's first constitution and its Declaration of Rights and, never one to shy from a public duty, even laid the cornerstone of the B&O Railroad. When he died at age ninety-five, he was the last remaining signer of the Declaration.

THE WHITE HOUSE AND CATHOLICS

John F. Kennedy was famously the first Catholic president, but Catholics have been connected in various ways to the White House throughout America's history. Elected to represent all Americans, presidents have pushed aside misgivings about Catholicism while occasionally still pushing away from them.

John Adams, the second president, was from an old line of austere Congregationalist New Englanders. Yet his presidency enlarged his sympathies. After his presidency ended in 1801, he wrote: "Ask me not whether I am Catholic, or Protestant, Calvinist or Arminian. As far as they are Christians, I wish to be a fellow disciple with them all."

Our third president, Thomas Jefferson, a deist, was initially accommodating to Catholicism — but his tolerance had its limits when it came to his own family. Before becoming president, he served as a diplomat in France and enrolled his beloved daughter Martha in a convent. Ignoring the shrill criticisms of Protestants in America, he believed a Catholic education was best for her. Then Martha decided she wanted to be a nun and wrote to her father to tell him she planned to convert. A miffed Jefferson rode his carriage to the door of the abbey and whisked away Martha and his other daughter, Maria. They never returned.

MRS. THOMAS M. RANDOLPH.

The initial First Lady with a Catholic upbringing was Louisa Catherine Adams, the wife of John Quincy Adams, elected president in 1825. Born in London to an Anglican family, she was taken to France by her father and educated in a convent. Unlike the wealthy French girls there, she disdained balls and dancing and spent hours on end at Mass or in the chapel in silent adoration before the crucifix. Her faith was close to her heart. She was traumatized by being brought back to England and forced to attend an Anglican church. She often fainted during services and repeatedly had to be carried out of the church.

Andrew Jackson, a swaggering, rough-hewed populist who was not shy about breaking traditions and making his own, brought Catholicism directly into the White House. Mary Anne Lewis was the charming daughter of a Jackson supporter, Major William Lewis. Jackson tried to play matchmaker with Mary Anne and his adopted son. After that predictably fizzled, Mary Anne fell in love with French diplomat Alphonse Pageot at a White House Christmas party. Jackson arranged their Catholic wedding at the White House on November 29, 1832. Fr.

William Matthews of St. Patrick Church in Washington presided. A year later, in another ceremony that had Protestant tongues wagging in Washington, the priest baptized Baby Pageot in the White House.

President John Tyler is barely remembered, but his wife's unexpected religious conversion decades after his presidency shocked 1870s America. Julia Gardiner Tyler, his second wife, had been a nonpracticing Episcopalian for most of her life. An age-old story: She turned to religion for succor as she dealt with family discord and financial troubles, not to mention a society still reeling from the ravages of the cataclysmic Civil War. She rigorously studied the theology and history of Catholicism and became a Catholic in 1872. Newspapers nationwide wrote of her startling, nearly scandalous, conversion. The stories were credited with easing acceptance of Catholics. Tyler also became a flashpoint for women facing their own personal troubles. They wrote to her seeking guidance about Catholicism, and she responded with literature, pamphlets, or personal letters. She was careful to tell others she freely chose Catholicism, whose most visible members were dogged by ugly rumors and suspicions. "No priest or nun had anything to do with it [her conversion]," she wrote. "It was simply from my own conviction of it being the best and truest religion as well as real Christianity."

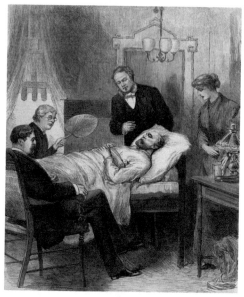

James Garfield came to understand and appreciate Catholicism as a soldier during the Civil War. His roommate was Major General William Rosecrans, a devout Catholic eager to share his faith. The major often brought a priest friend to the quarters, and the soldier solemnly knelt in prayer before going to bed. Garfield began attending Mass with Rosecrans and even had the priest say Mass in his room. Getting cozy with Catholics then could dismay family and friends, and Garfield anticipated his mother's concern. "I hope you are not alarmed about my becoming Catholic," he wrote to her in a letter. Then he could not resist chiding her: "You ought to be glad that I take the time to think and talk about religion at all. I have no doubt the Catholics have been greatly slandered." His affinity for Catholics did not impede his political rise. He was elected to Congress in 1862 and, in 1881, was elected president. Six months later, an assassin shot him. As he lay dying in the White House, an Irish Catholic maid took it upon herself to help his immortal soul. She quietly sprinkled holy water into his milk before he died.

President Calvin Coolidge was famously reticent, but the words he spoke to Catholic leaders near the White House tamped down a fierce display of anti-Catholicism. As immigrants swarmed to America in the 1920s, the Ku Klux Klan gained in numbers and political power. The Klan gathered in Washington and marched in their white robes in a huge parade. They invited Coolidge to review them, but he refused. Instead, in a park just behind the White House lawn, he warmly addressed a large contingent of Catholic bishops and priests who were in the city for a conference.

By the mid-twentieth century, Catholics had begun to lose their outsider status. They had fought and died on the battlefields of World War II like other Americans and had distinguished themselves in boardrooms and on ball fields. The papacy was seen less as a foreign menace and more as a benevolent force. On a world tour in 1959, President Dwight D. Eisenhower met with the new Pope, John XXIII, at the Vatican.

At the White House itself, Catholics were also kosher. First Lady Mamie Eisenhower, though a devout Presbyterian, was cognizant of the spiritual needs of the Catholics on the White House staff. Between two rooms of the White House kitchen, she had a plaque placed on the wall with a statue and a prayer to the Blessed Mother.

Ronald Reagan might well have become a Catholic if not for happenstance during his childhood. His father was a churchgoing Irish

Catholic, but his mother was a churchgoing Protestant. What to do? Young Ron's older brother, Neil, tagged along with their father to the Catholic Mass in their small Illinois town, while Ron attended the First Christian Church with his mother. His father's faith remained a part

of his life, at least his polit- ical life. President Reagan was close to many Catholic religious leaders. After his recovery from being shot in 1981, he began a remarkable spiritual friendship with Cardinal Terence Cooke of New York. The president once confided to Cooke that he believed his recovery ob- ligated him to live for others. Cooke smartly replied that during the president's hospi- tal stay, "God was sitting on your shoulders."

A myriad of forces con- verged to put Barack Obama in the White House. Part of that fabric of chance and consequence were a handful of Catholic churches on the South Side of Chicago.

In the mid-1980s, Obama moved to Chicago to do community or- ganizing for the Developing Communities Project, supported by ten Catholic churches on the Black South Side. The mostly impoverished South Side was reeling from the steel-mill closings. Jerry Kellman, who grew up Jewish and converted to Catholicism in the 1980s, hired Obama to pull South Siders together and advocate for change and for more government funding and investment in their neighborhoods.

Obama met with public-housing residents and other disadvantaged people to listen to their concerns and strategized with priests and nuns. He did not enjoy much concrete success in his two years, but he learned a great deal. He began to hone his understanding of local communities, the possibilities of political change, and the importance of relationships in effecting change.

Working alongside Kellman was invaluable too. Kellman was the first of his many mentors and "may well have played the most influential role in Obama's life outside of his family," according to journalist David Remnick. Convinced he needed to be less of an outsider and needed better credentials to effect change, Obama left the job after a couple of years to attend Harvard Law School. The White House was twenty years away.

THE LIBERTY BELL

The famous Liberty Bell, commonly associated with the Revolutionary War and the fight for freedom, actually was forged many years before the war to commemorate religious freedom in Pennsylvania. The massive bell cracked the first time it was rung. Its replacement rang for decades in a historical Catholic church in Philadelphia — until, ironically, it was destroyed in an anti-Catholic riot.

William Penn founded the colony of Pennsylvania in 1701 as a "holy experiment" in religious coexistence. His charter guaranteed religious freedom, not granted by other colonies. The City of Brotherly Love pioneered religious harmony among those of persecuted faiths, such as Quakers, Catholics, and Jews, as well as mainline Protestants.

Catholics found a haven in Pennsylvania. When St. Joseph Church was established in Philadelphia in 1733, it was the sole place in the entire English-speaking world where the Mass was permitted by law. Catholics could hardly believe it and didn't quite trust the guarantee. In its early decades, the parish kept a low profile, and priests cautiously went about the city in Quaker garb.

Fifty years after its founding, the colony celebrated its charter and its unique religious freedom. In 1751, the Pennsylvania Assembly approved a two-thousand-pound bell to be purchased from Whitechapel

Bell Foundry in London. It would be rung in the new state house, later called Independence Hall.

After that historical bell cracked when tested, city leaders ordered a new bell from Whitechapel. The cracked bell was given to a local foundry to be recast. The recast bell was ready first and was dubbed the "Sister Bell." It was placed in the bell tower at the state house. When Whitechapel's replacement bell arrived, it was attached to the clock at the state house. Both bells rang for special occasions. They rang loud and long on July 8, 1776, to accompany a defiant public reading of the Declaration of Independence

During renovations of Independence Hall in the late 1820s, city officials transferred the Sister Bell from Independence Hall to Olde St. Augustine Church in Philadelphia. The church was precious to Catholics. Two Irish friars sent by the Vatican in 1796 to minister to the city's growing Catholic population had laid its cornerstone. Donors to the church included George Washington; John Barry, the father of the U.S. Navy; and Thomas Fitzsimons, a signer of the Constitution.

The parish's founding represented the first permanent establishment of the Augustinian Order in the United States. The church had a library with three thousand books, the largest theological collection in the cultured city. St. Augustine Academy opened in 1811 as one of the first Catholic secondary schools in America, and Villanova University eventually sprang from it.

By 1838, St. Augustine was the city's largest church, with three thousand parishioners. Catholic immigrants were a growing force, and this aroused the nativists — white, U.S.-born Americans who felt threatened by immigrants. The match that lit the flame was when the bishop asked the school board to let Catholic students use a Catholic version of the Bible instead of the King James version. The suspicious public accused the Church of trying to eliminate the Bible in public schools.

Irish Catholics and nativists fought in the streets. Eleven nativists and two Catholics were killed. Inflamed by the major newspapers, implacably hostile to immigrants, the nativists retaliated. They set fire to Catholic institutions and homes. On May 8, 1844, St. Augustine's was burned to the ground. Only the wall behind the altar was left standing.

On it, in charred gilt letters, remained the words "The Lord Seeth."

The library and its books were lost. Amid the rubble, the Sister Bell, symbol of Penn's dream of freedom, lay burned and smashed, destroyed by the flames.

Three years later, the Sister Bell was recast, though greatly reduced in size. It was sent to Villanova College. Until 1917, it hung in a locust tree and was used to call the students to class, chapel, and meals. Today the historic bell sits in the Augustinian Heritage Room at Villanova University and can be seen by appointment.

THE GETTYSBURG PRIEST

Lincoln was right when he spoke at Gettysburg: No one can hallow that ground. The brave men who died there hallowed it. But for Catho-

lics, there is on the grounds a statue of a priest who is long remembered for offering comfort and a final blessing to Union troops before they flung themselves into battle.

Fr. William Corby, the son of an Irish immigrant, studied for the priesthood and then taught at Notre Dame. He left the university in 1861 to serve as chaplain of the Eighty-Eighth New York Infantry, a mostly Irish Catholic unit. The brigade had already suffered great losses before Gettysburg.

On July 2, 1863, fearful of the further death his brigade would face, Corby gave general absolution, customary in Europe but unheard of in the United States, to the 500 remaining men in his brigade. Twenty-seven of them were killed at Gettysburg, 109 were wounded, many grievously, and sixty-two were listed as missing.

Corby's stirring memoir of the Irish Brigade became a bestseller. Corby also made a huge impact at Notre Dame, where he served as president from 1866 to 1872 and 1877 to 1881. He began construction of Sacred Heart Church, known today as the Basilica of the Sacred Heart. He also rebuilt the school's old main building, destroyed by fire. His new Main Building is the one with the famous Golden Dome.

Corby was a popular, colorful figure on campus. Students and teachers once presented him with the gift of a beautiful black horse and, when he retired, a matching carriage.

There are several theories as to why the Notre Dame football team is known as the Fighting Irish. One story is that the name followed the chaplain of the Irish soldiers back to South Bend. A second theory relates to the anti-Catholicism of the early twentieth century. Fans of rival teams taunted the Notre Dame players as dirty, uncouth, brawling Irish immigrants. Coach Knute Rockne decided to take the taunts and turn them to his advantage, and the players took pride in their ferocity.

Corby died in 1897. In 1910, his statue was dedicated — the first for a non-general at Gettysburg. He is perched on a rock and blessing his beloved troops. A copy of the statue stands outside Corby Hall at Notre Dame, not far from where he is buried at peaceful Holy Cross Cemetery on campus.

CASEY JONES

Pony Express riders captured the imagination of Americans in the 1840s, and in the first part of the twentieth century, airplane pilots soared to acclaim and wonder. Almost forgotten now is the fascination with train engineers in the 1800s. Trains were hailed for ushering in a modern era, and the men at the helm of locomotive cars were exalted as fearless heroes. No engineer stood taller than Casey Jones, celebrated in "The Ballad of Casey Jones." According to legend, Jones died with one hand on the train's whistle and the other hand on the brake.

Born John Luther Jones in Missouri in 1863, he took on a new first name when his family moved to Cayce, Kentucky. He scuffled as a telegrapher, brakeman, and fireman before finding himself when he was transferred by the railroad to Jackson, Tennessee, a railroad hub. There he boarded with a Mrs. Brady, a practicing Catholic, and fell in love with her daughter Janie. He was baptized before marrying Janie and settled into the role of dedicated family man and trustworthy engineer.

Jones was an engineer for the Illinois Central Railroad when he volunteered to take the place of a sick engineer on a route from Memphis. As his train rounded a blind curve, a disabled train loomed just ahead. Casey reversed the throttle, hit the brakes, and sounded a blast on the whistle. "Jump! Sim, jump," he yelled to his fireman. The train plowed through a caboose and two cars of corn and hay. Thanks to Casey's quick thinking and selflessness, the passengers on the train and Sim suffered only minor injuries. Casey was found dead beside the tracks.

Casey was buried at St. Mary's Cathedral in Jackson, where he and Janie had been married. Wallace Saunders, a Black railroad worker, wrote the poignant ballad about Jones sung first at vaudeville shows. Johnny Cash and others later recorded it. Radio and TV shows further spread Jones's popularity. The Casey home in Jackson became a museum.

Imitating his Savior, Casey laid down his life for others. Saunders's poignant salute to his comrade ensures Jones's enduring fame:

Caller called Jones about half past four
Jones kissed his wife at the station door
Climbed into the cab with his orders in his hand
Says, "This is my trip to the Promised Land."

"God Bless America"

"The Star Spangled Banner" is America's national anthem. But our de facto anthem is "God Bless America." It's sung at ball games, in churches, and on July 4. After September 11, its popularity soared even higher. On that terrible day, U.S. House and Senate members delivered a stirring spontaneous rendition on the Capitol steps. In the days following, it rang out on the stages on Broadway, in the pews of the National Cathedral, and in the balcony of the New York Stock Exchange.

The song burst onto the scene in 1938 when Kate Smith performed it on her radio show. It became the rallying song for the United States during World War II. It's hard to overstate the song's popularity and emotional power over Americans or how Smith was synonymous with the song. She became a symbol of the land she extolled. When President Roosevelt introduced her to King George VI of England, he said, "This is Kate Smith. This is America."

Born in 1907, Smith grew up in Washington with a Catholic father and a Protestant mother. She attended Presbyterian Sunday school and sang at church socials when she was six. She was a true prodigy. She sang for World War I soldiers stationed in Washington when she was nine. She once hopped on a table to dance and sing for legendary general John Pershing. When she was done, the general took off a medal he was wearing and pinned it to her dress. "You must keep singing, child," the famous general told her.

Her first big break in show business happened thanks to a priest. As a teenager, she sang in local vaudeville shows and at shows held at churches. When she sang and danced at St. Aloysius Church in Washington, a priest who loved the theater was in the audience. He introduced her to a theatrical producer he knew, and the sixteen-year-old Smith ended up on Broadway.

By 1938, Smith was a star. *The Kate Smith Hour* was radio's most popular show. That year was a dismal time. The Great Depression still held sway. War in Europe hung in the air. Smith asked her friend Irving

Berlin for a song to raise the spirits of the nation.

A Jewish immigrant, Berlin was America's most prolific and beloved songwriter. He wrote his first version of "God Bless America" in 1918 when he was a soldier at Camp Upton on Long Island. The camp's general asked him to write a musical revue. Berlin dutifully cranked out "Yip, Yip, Yaphank," a zesty Ziegfeld-style show. "God Bless America" didn't make the final cut. Berlin deemed it too schmaltzy and shelved it away in his desk drawer.

Smith's request led Berlin to scribble out a song he titled "Thanks, America." He tried to express his heartfelt devotion to his adopted land. But he tore it up in a fit of pique. The words didn't ring true to him.

Then Berlin remembered the song he had discarded at Camp Upton. There was one problem. That version of "God Bless America" was a rousing, backslapping ode to America. It was almost a call to arms. He wanted a song of peace, clean of any political connotations. So he made crucial changes, subtle but significant. The original lyric was: "Stand beside her, and guide her / To the right with a light from above / Make her victorious on land and foam." The new verse was: "Stand beside her, and guide her / Thru the night with a light from above / From the mountains, to the prairies / To the oceans, white with foam."

Smith first performed "God Bless America" on Sunday, November 11, 1938. That was Armistice Day, today's Veteran's Day. The song was a sensation, and demand for its sheet music went through the roof.

Berlin generously donated the song's royalties to the Boy Scouts and Girl Scouts of America. That sum became millions over time. During the war, Smith's voice and Berlin's tune pried open wallets. Smith's radio appeals generated an incredible $600 million in war-bond sales.

Smith was a public figure who enthusiastically embraced who she was. Her legions of fans could quickly describe her in two or three ways. She was a large woman. She good-naturedly once told *Lady's Circle* she always had "a tendency to put it on" and, as a young person, had taken a secret oath not to let her size interfere with anything she wanted to do. She was refreshingly blunt and self-accepting: "I know I'm fat and my hair is straight, but I can sing!"

She also was deeply patriotic. "When I sing 'God Bless America,' it's my personal message to God for allowing me to be born an American."

Finally, she was upfront about her faith. One of her greatest thrills, she often said, was a private audience with Pope Paul VI. On the road, she often went to Mass. Her Mass attendance went on for decades without her formally taking up the Faith. A series of misfortunes, one after another, in 1964 led her to take the leap.

Smith suffered a kidney-stone attack, broke her foot, overcame a bad case of bronchitis, and lost a good friend to a heart attack. Next came the sudden death of Ted Collins, her agent, lawyer, partner, and "dearest friend." Just sixty-four, he died of a massive heart attack. Smith was devastated. His funeral Mass was held at a Catholic church in New York, and Fr. Albert Salmon of St. Agnes Church in Lake Placid consoled Smith.

Things got even worse for Smith. While in seclusion at the home of a friend, she somehow fell through a plate-glass shower door. She lost a great amount of blood, was rushed to the hospital, and had a long recuperation.

Smith did a lot of soul-searching and decided God was trying to tell her something. She took instruction in the Catholic Faith, and Father Salmon, who had given Collins last rites, baptized her and gave her First Communion. From then on, whenever she was in Lake Placid, she attended Mass at St. Agnes, and parishioners delighted in hearing her sing the hymns in her wondrous contralto voice.

Ravaged by diabetes, Smith died in 1986, four years after receiving from President Reagan the Presidential Medal of Freedom, the nation's highest civilian honor.

The Kate Smith USA Friends Club, formed in 1967 with many Catholic members, renamed itself the Kate Smith Commemorative Society. A priest from New York headed it for years.

Smith's will left $25,000 to "my dear friend" Cardinal Terence Cooke, the archbishop of New York. But he had died in 1983. So those funds and another $340,000 went to St. Agnes Church and Uihlein Mercy Center in Lake Placid. Father Salmon received $10,000. Smith left the rest of America her signature song, a priceless tribute to their country.

THE ALAMO

"Remember the Alamo!" was the battle cry of Texans, avenging the fall of the fortress. Today the Alamo is a potent symbol of American freedom. Few remember that, for most of its history, the Alamo was a Catholic mission, part of the largest chain of missions in North America.

Mission San Antonio de Valero was one of thirty-six missions founded by Spain in Texas between 1680 and 1793, five of which are in San Antonio. The Franciscans came to convert Native Americans. The soldiers and settlers accompanying them were dispatched by Spanish rulers to expand their nation's empire.

Each mission was a self-contained city, including a church, living quarters for priests, workshops, warehouses, granaries, farm fields, and ranchlands. The converted Indians lived in a safely enclosed area, where they grew crops and raised cattle. They also attended as many as three religious services each day.

The missions eventually declined because Spain lost interest in them as military assets. European diseases ravaged the population, and the Apache and Comanche tribes grew increasingly hostile. Spain finally gave up on the missions in 1793 and secularized the property. The land was distributed to local residents.

In the early 1800s, troops lodged in the abandoned chapel of the former San Antonio de Valero mission. Because it stood in a grove of cottonwood trees, the soldiers called their new fort "El Alamo," the Spanish word for "cottonwood," and also in honor of Alamo de Parras, their hometown in Mexico.

In 1835, during Texas's war for independence from Mexico, a group of Texan volunteers captured the fort. February 1836 witnessed the famous battle for the Alamo, in which the Mexican army wiped out a vastly outnumbered Texan contingent, which included Davy Crockett.

The property had been in disrepair even before the deadly, destructive battle. The Church sold the decayed buildings to the state of Texas in the early 1880s, and in 1905, the Daughters of the Republic of Texas took over custodial care of the Alamo. The state again assumed formal control in 2015.

Preservation work was done over the years, and it will continue. The famous Alamo building, the one seen on postcards, is the former mission church that was never finished. The other four missions in San Antonio are active Catholic parishes with regular Masses. The Alamo, of course, has achieved near-sacred status in the American imagination.

RED CROSS CHURCH

The cornerstone of Saint Mary of Sorrows Church in Fairfax Station, Virginia, was laid in 1858. Four years later, a fierce battle of the Civil War raged around it, and the horrific suffering that occurred inside the church led to the founding of the American Red Cross.

Until the church in Fairfax Station was built, the pastor of St. Mary's in Alexandria ministered to local Catholics. Irish immigrants worked for the nearby railroad, and the priest said Mass in boxcars parked a

quarter mile from where the church was eventually built.

Because of the railroad depot, Fairfax Station was vital to both the Union and Confederate armies. Violent skirmishes erupted regularly in the early part of the war. The town changed hands multiple times.

Jesuit Fr. Peter Kroes, a native of the Netherlands, stood by his parishioners at St. Mary and backed the Southern cause. When Union troops occupied the town, the priest refused to take an oath of allegiance to the Union. He lost his right to bless legally binding marriages, so he sent his engaged parishioners to Washington to be married.

Tensions continued to mount as the war went on. Fr. Joseph Bixio, Kroes's assistant, was suspected as a spy and brought before Gen. William T. Sherman. The priest kept his poise and convinced the general that his work was entirely spiritual, dodging the hangman's noose.

The fierce Battle of Manassas was fought over three days in late August 1862. It began when about 35,000 Union troops marched from the federal capital in Washington to strike a Confederate force of 20,000 along a small river known as Bull Run. It was the first major battle of the war, and the casualties shocked both sides. Union Maj. Gen. John Pope's troops suffered 14,462 killed, wounded, or missing. Gen. Robert E. Lee's forces lost 9,474.

Clara Barton rushed to Fairfax from Alexandria to tend to the wounded. When the war had begun, eighteen months earlier, wounded soldiers were hauled to Washington. Supplies were meager. Aid was haphazard. A forty-one-year-old clerk in the Government Patent Office, Barton, not affiliated with any aid group, took it upon herself to nurse the soldiers. A complex person, Barton was independent, demanding, and vain about her looks, especially her hair. She suffered bouts of debilitating depression. Yet she also could be utterly charming, and when under great distress, she was fearless and tireless.

She solicited donations and provided food, clothing, and bedding for the soldiers. She also offered personal support. She read to the soldiers, wrote letters for them, listened to their personal problems, and prayed with them.

Barton realized that if things were this bad behind the lines, conditions on the battlefields must be immeasurably worse. She began prodding government leaders to allow her to do more, and the army gave her passes to bring services and supplies directly to the battlefields.

In a battle in northern Virginia in 1862, she appeared at a field hospital at midnight with a wagonload of supplies drawn by a four-mule team. The surgeon on duty wrote later, "I thought that night if heaven ever sent out an angel, she must be one — her assistance was so timely." Thereafter she was known throughout the North as "the Angel of the Battlefield."

The Union was losing the Battle of Manassas. As troops began retreating, a field hospital was moved inside St. Mary's. Pews were ripped out and set on a hill outside the church, and some of the wounded were laid on them. They had to wait for food and ammunition to be unloaded from the nearby railyard before they could be placed in the trains and evacuated.

For three interminable days and nights, Barton worked with the doctors to care for the wounded at the church. The suffering was unimaginable. The Confederate army was making a final, decisive push toward the church. Barton, other volunteers, and the doctors stayed until the last of the men were evacuated. Barton narrowly escaped, too, and she watched from the windows of the last train as the Confederates captured Fairfax Station and set fire to the depot.

The incredibly intense experience at the church convinced Barton of the need for a civilian society in times of crisis. In 1881, she realized her dream when she founded the American Red Cross, which she led for twenty-three years.

The soldiers buried in the churchyard during the Civil War were later moved to Arlington National Cemetery. A new St. Mary's was built in 1980. The historical church, still standing, is used for weekday Masses and weddings. A plaque honoring Barton's heroism sits on the side of the road. Tradition has it that the church's pews were installed after the war at the order of President U. S. Grant. He ordered restitution when he learned that Union soldiers had ripped them out to care for the wounded.

GROUNDHOG DAY

No holiday can seem less likely to have a religious origin than Groundhog Day, and no holiday is as peculiarly American. Really, does anyone outside the United States know who Punxsutawney Phil is? Yet the holiday owes its origin to the

February 2 feast of Candlemas, which commemorates Mary's presentation of her Son in the Temple forty days after his birth. The elderly

prophet Simeon took Jesus in his arms and announced that he was to be the "light for the revelation to the Gentiles" (Lk 2:32).

From that passage emerged a folk belief that the weather on February 2 had a predictive value. Whether the day was sunny or cloudy would determine a lengthier winter or early spring. The Germans were the ones who dragged a badger or a hedgehog into the equation. But when they immigrated to Pennsylvania in the eighteenth century, they discovered no evidence of those two animals. So, because the Native Americans considered the groundhog to be a wise animal, the Germans adopted that furry critter to be their Candlemas prognosticator.

THE DOLLAR BILL

What is more American than the dollar bill? Well, turn it over and take a good look at the image of an eye above a pyramid on the left half. The "Eye of Providence" was originally a Catholic symbol, signifying God's compassionate watchfulness over humanity. The earliest examples are in religious art of the Renaissance period. The symbol is still found today in churches in the United States and Europe.

In reality, however, the Eye of Providence, as eye-catching as it is, was eventually co-opted by other groups and for other purposes, and its religious significance had faded by the time America was settled. It was incorporated into the design of the dollar bill because the Eye of Providence, hovering above a pyramid, was the reverse of the Great Seal of the United States, adopted way back in 1782.

Thomas Jefferson, Benjamin Franklin, and John Adams proposed ideas for the seal, but, as gifted as they were, their forte was revolutionary thinking, not art. So Charles Thomson, secretary of the Continental Congress, came up with the pyramid and the Eye of Providence. The pyramid symbolizes strength and duration. Its thirteen levels represent the thirteen colonies. The pyramid is unfinished — a subtle nod to the notion that our nation was a work in progress.

VI

HOLY (ROCK 'N')
ROLLERS

In the 1960s, before it went mainstream, rock music was antiestablishment. Rock musicians sported long hair and unkempt clothes, scorned the values of their elders, and sang about love, freedom, and other passions of youth. Respectable folks wouldn't be caught dead at a rock concert. So it's easy to imagine that a modern-day Jesus, who mingled with prostitutes, tax collectors, and Samaritans, might have donned his Levis, not bothered to trim his beard and long hair, and stuck out his thumb to hitchhike to Woodstock.

That image, whether appealing or off-putting, sells short and obscures the value of popular music — indeed, all music and creativity. Singing has been described as "praying twice," because it's a portal to the divine. A good song is transcendent. It transports us to an unthinking place of contentment and gratitude, to a cessation of ordinary time and events, and to a sweet, unbidden arrival of truth and beauty. A good song is nothing less than *kairos*, God's time. What pleases the ear and soothes the heart are sound waves of the kingdom. Einstein, who explained the entire universe, got to the root of the magic of music. After hearing a renowned violinist play, he gushed, "Thank you. You have once again proved to me that there is a God in heaven."

Catholics believe in the sacredness of life. The Incarnation brought God to us directly. We experience God not only in church but in our daily lives. Holiness can belong not only to priests and to people in the pews but also to musicians and lovers of music. God does not linger behind a scrim or play a cosmic game of hide-and-seek. He joins us at the table when we dine with our families, plops himself down in a chair in the conference room at work meetings, and nods his head to the tunes we listen to on Spotify.

If it seems a stretch to find exalted themes in popular, seemingly pedestrian music, consider the stories Jesus told. He was attuned to the "popular culture" of his day. In his parables, he spoke of shepherds, bread and wine, seeds and trees. He didn't teach about God using esoteric theological terms but located God in ordinary events and routines.

The Church gets it. At a Eucharistic congress in 1997 in Bologna, Italy, John Paul II once tapped his foot to the songs of Bob Dylan. The scruffy rock icon was the special guest of the pope, who later addressed the mostly youthful audience. Referring to Dylan and one of his most well-known songs, the pope remarked, "He says the answer to the questions of your lives is blowing in the wind. This is true, in the wind that is the breath and voice of the Spirit."

THE BEATLES

In 1956, Liverpool, heavily bombed by the Germans, was still blighted by rubble. Rationing had ended only two years earlier. Hopes were low and money was scarce. In this drab, beaten-down time, two teenage boys on their way to school met each day on the No. 86 bus. The older one, bright-eyed and smart, got on first. The younger one, who boarded at the next stop, was quiet and introspective. They bonded over music and later formed a band.

The younger one became interested in Eastern mysticism and wrote songs about love and peace. The other one eschewed formal religion. Still, he wrote what is probably the greatest spiritual rock song.

Both lads were baptized Catholics.

We are talking about George Harrison and Paul McCartney, of course.

It's ludicrous to call the mop-tops a Catholic band. But it's also wrong to discount the spirituality woven into their music and their lives or to deny that their songs are often compatible or even congruent with Catholicism.

Born in 1943, Harrison's mother, like so many others in Liverpool, had her roots in Ireland. She was a practicing Catholic. Baby George was christened at Our Lady of Good Help Church. He went to Mass with his mother and made his first confession and his first Communion. When it came time for confirmation, George, a mediocre student who often was defiant and sullen, opted out. "I'm not going to bother with that. I'll just confirm myself later on," he said.

It's no surprise that Harrison turned away from religion. After the war, the English left the churches in droves. Anyone who went to church was regarded as exceptional, almost eccentric. The wonder is not that the Beatles were not churchgoers but that, amid a secular culture, they pursued higher truths. In this unexpected, ironic way, they rebelled against the prevailing materialism.

The Beatles evolved from teenage sensations, churning out simple-minded pop ditties such as "I Want to Hold Your Hand," to sophisticated musicians exploring social troubles such as ennui and alienation in "A Day in the Life," "Nowhere Man," and "Eleanor Rigby." While other popular bands, such as the Rolling Stones, celebrated conflict, brute physicality, and nihilism, the Beatles seemed to rise above the fray and lean into peace and community. "The love you take is equal to the love you make," they sang.

Harrison, who distrusted and disdained authority from a young age, did not hide his dislike of the official Church and made disparaging remarks about the papacy. He saw it cynically as a money grab. Restless and inquisitive, he also became disenchanted with the adulation and wealth that came with being a Beatle.

At the height of their fame in 1968, the Beatles famously visited India to explore Eastern mysticism. It was Harrison's idea. Since he was young, he had been interested in what life was really about. "George himself is no mystery," said John Lennon. "But the mystery inside George is immense." At one point, Harrison rose with the sun and meditated nearly the entire day. He became a kind of honorary Hare Krishna.

Harrison wrote relatively few songs for the Beatles. "Long, Long, Long" on the White Album was, he explained, a song to God. As a solo artist, Harrison merged his spirituality with his songwriting. His top hits, "What Is Life," "All Things Must Pass," and "Give Me Love, Give Me Peace on Earth," reflect his deepest concerns.

"My Sweet Lord" fused Eastern spirituality with Christian Gospel. The chorus jumps from "Hallelujah" to "Hare Krishna." Near the end of the song, Harrison chants a series of exotic names. "What the hell are all these guys?" a bandmate asked. "They're all gods," Harrison replied. "Way too many gods, George," said the bandmate.

McCartney went to church on occasion as a boy. He sang in the church choir. But his identity as a Catholic never took hold. When he was hospitalized as an eleven-year-old, the nun on duty asked him his religion. "I don't know," he replied.

Charming, unflappable, and forever boyishly handsome, he considered himself agnostic. If ever a bloke could get by without God, it would seem to be he. Yet he has reverted to that old spiritual standby —

prayer — while in distress. When his wife, Linda, had to deliver their second child by Caesarean in 1971, he recalls, "I sat next door in my green apron praying like mad."

Linda died of cancer in 1998 at age fifty-five. "Let It Be," McCartney's great spiritual anthem, was played at the funeral. He wrote it in 1969 during an extremely distressing period. His relationship with his songwriting partner, John Lennon, was crumbling. The breakup of the Beatles loomed. His own drug use was taking a toll.

McCartney wrote the song after he dreamed of his mother, who had died a decade earlier, when he was a boy. Her passing had devastated him. "It was so great to see her because that's a wonderful thing about dreams: you actually are reunited with that person for a second. There you are and you appear to both be physically together again."

"It was so wonderful for me, and she was very reassuring. In the dream she said, 'It will be alright.' I'm not sure if she used the words, 'Let it be,' but that was the gist of her advice. It was, 'Don't worry too much. It will turn out OK.'"

Mary was his mum's name, so that's why he invoked the name of Mary. Listeners assume he meant *the* Mary. "Mother Mary makes it a quasi-religious thing, so you can take it that way. I don't mind," McCartney told biographer Barry Miles. "I'm quite happy if people want to use it to shore up their faith. I have no problem with that. I think it's a great thing to have faith of any sort, particularly in the world we live in."

McCartney is also pleased that fans appreciate the Beatles' music for its optimism and hope. "Looking back on all the Beatles' work, I'm very glad that most of it was positive and has been a positive force. I always find it very fortunate that most of our songs were to do with peace and love and encourage people to do better and to have a better life," he said.

McCartney has shown a knack for honoring other people's faith and acknowledging the immortality of the soul. He did car karaoke with late-night host James Corden, who told McCartney how his dad, a musician, and his grandfather once excitedly played "Let It Be" for him. "If my grandad was here right now, he'd get an absolute kick out of this," Corden gushed. McCartney turned to him, smiled warmly and said, "He is."

The Beatles' most visible encounter with religion was not positive. John Lennon ignited a firestorm in 1967 when he said the Beatles were more popular than Jesus. Even before he said that, the quartet were shocked at the religiosity of Americans. Lennon was forced to apologize, even though he clearly was misunderstood. He admired Jesus for his ethic of love and brotherhood. The Beatles probably *were* more popular than Jesus in religiously somnolent England. If anything, Lennon was chiding Americans for their over-the-top obsession with a rock band.

Like Paul, John lost his mother as a boy. Unlike Paul, he struggled mightily to find inner peace. During a time when his relationships with his wife, Yoko, and his son, Julian, were strained and he suffered from drug and alcohol abuse, he quietly wrote a letter to televangelist Oral Roberts. "I want happiness. ... Explain to me what Christianity can do for me. Is it phony? Can He love me?" It was a startling admission — from a man with almost unmatched worldly success and fame and a disdain for institutions such as organized religion — that life can ring hollow without a spiritual grounding.

Ringo Starr, regarded as the "average Joe" in the band without the talent or depth of his three bandmates, also turned toward God as he aged. As he neared seventy, he told a reporter, "For me, God is in my life. I don't hide from that. I think the search has been on since the 1960s." When caught on camera in public, Ringo often makes the peace sign and shouts, "Peace and love!"

Lennon was shot outside his apartment building in New York on December 8, 1980, the feast of the Immaculate Conception. The next year, the Beatles came together for a tribute song for him; it was the first time the Beatles collaborated since their acrimonious breakup. "All Those Years Ago," mainly a Harrison creation, tells of a man who shouts "all about love" while being treated "like a dog." That is Lennon, no doubt. Society is guilty of something else too. "They've forgotten about God," Harrison sings. "He's the only reason we exist."

The Beatles' popularity did not bridge the generation gap of the time. Their long hair, drug use, and loud, fast music brought condemnation from some quarters, including the Church. Lennon's comment on Jesus in particular was not well received at the Vatican. But in 2010, the Vatican "forgave" the Beatles. The Vatican's official newspaper, *L'Osservatore Romano*, praised the group for their musical achievements. "They may not have been the best example for the youth of the day," the newspaper maintained. However, their "beautiful melodies changed music and continue to give pleasure." The band was a "precious jewel."

The Church even extended an olive branch over Lennon's remarks about Jesus. The Vatican newspaper excused his remark as the "boasting of an English working-class lad struggling to cope with unexpected success."

Fans knew the Beatles did not need forgiveness. They took from the band the love they made.

BRUCE SPRINGSTEEN

In his Broadway show in 2017, Bruce Springsteen sang songs and told stories to detail his journey from nervous boy to rock star to chastened older man. As he recounted in a soft, almost shy tone, his mother was doting and loving. His father was another story: a man of few words but many beers, drunk at night, alone in the gloom of a dark kitchen.

Bruce found his escape hatch when he was seven. It came in the form of swiveling hips, a snarled lip, and a beat with roots in Black music. Televised into Bruce's shotgun home in New Jersey, Elvis was a revelation on *The Ed Sullivan Show*. Bruce badgered his mom into renting a guitar, since an outright purchase was beyond their means.

Besides his father's depression, something else shadowed Bruce as a child. It literally hovered over the family. Sitting outside the window of their modest home was St. Rose of Lima Catholic Church and its rectory, convent, and school. His mom was a fervent believer, and Bruce attended a Catholic church and school and served as an altar boy.

He chafed under the stern discipline of the nuns at the school. He loathed its literal uniformity — "the green blazers, green ties, green trousers, green socks!" But the nuns and their teachings fired his imagination. Swirling about him was God and the devil, grace and sin. Bruce learned there was more to the world than meets the eye. There was something sacred and eternal beyond the ordinary and the mundane.

From his home, he witnessed weddings and funerals. When the church bells rang for the former, he and his sister rushed out of the house with paper bags, collecting the rice or throwing rice gathered from other weddings. After funerals, they scavenged the fallen flowers. Weddings and funerals — limousines and hearses, crowds of smiling, clapping throngs and rows of silent, tearful mourners. He came to un-

derstand and appreciate the bittersweet cycle of life.

Springsteen found salvation in rock music. Church was not cool. As a typically rebellious youth, he consciously wanted to reject his faith. Yet as much as he wanted to push it away, it hovered over him.

Near the end of his Broadway show, Springsteen reminisces about his troubled late father, and his beloved bandmate, the late Clarence Clemons. He somberly reflects on their immortal souls. He then abruptly pivots to his faith: "You know what they say about Catholics — yeah, there is no getting out. They got you. They got you when the getting was good. They did the work hard, but they did it well." After two hours of profane language and songs and stories rife with struggle and sin, Springsteen startlingly, solemnly, and movingly prays the Our Father.

Springsteen acknowledges his artistic debt to his religious upbringing. "In Catholicism, there existed the poetry, danger, and darkness that reflected my imagination and my inner self," he writes in his autobiography. His faith, along with his family and neighborhood, animated his music. "Most of my writing is emotionally autobiographical. I've learned you've got to pull things up that mean something to you in order for them to mean something to your audience."

Springsteen is a self-acknowledged contradiction. He admits he represents the working-class stiff, yet he never worked a nine-to-five job in his life. He was born to run and fled his "death-trap, suicide-rap" hometown, yet he ended up living ten minutes from where he grew up. To these contradictions can be added another: He sings of the streets and the down-and-dirty bid to survive tedious jobs and dysfunctional families, but he delves into the struggles of the soul, the quest to find meaning.

Catholicism is not just a spark to Springsteen's creativity but a core of his identity. He may spout slews of profanities in his shows and seek redemption in girls, cars, and guitars in his songs. But he knows in his heart, as when he recites the Lord's Prayer, some things are just beyond our control — thy will be done. The Boss understands he's not the Boss.

"Once you're a Catholic, you're always a Catholic," he writes. "I don't often participate in my religion, but I know somewhere deep inside I'm still on the team."

Springsteen sings of wounded Americans. His heroes are outsiders and losers, the wounded and the vulnerable, the seekers and the wanderers, the dissatisfied and the disillusioned. His characters inhabit the everyday world — in crummy jobs, troubled relationships, and those soul-crushing moments of doubt and dismay. His characters are weighed down by bitter circumstances — or, on occasion, uplifted in moments of transcendence.

Springsteen once gave a benefit concert at his old grade school. At the start of his set, he joked, "I'll take care of the sin. Father McCarron [the pastor] will take care of the redemption." That's the trickster in Springsteen, denying what he's up to. Redemption lies at the heart of his vast songbook. "I believe in a promised land," he roars in one of his most iconic songs.

Religious imagery suffuses his songs. A tribute to the firefighters who perished in the Twin Towers, "The Rising," puts forth a vision of a self-sacrificing death followed by a heavenly reward. The spirituality is front and center: "the cross of my calling," spirits, precious blood, Mary in the garden, holy pictures, and, at last, dancing in a light-filled sky, wearin' the cross of my calling.

"Thunder Road" tells of a man who has had his ups and down with his girlfriend but pays a visit to set things right. He references crosses, praying, a savior, redemption, and a promised land. A relationship is about a boy and a girl, but it's also the canvas for a spiritual journey.

Springsteen is not a theologian. He does not write carefully crafted religious treatises. Rather, he unspools stories with a spiritual resonance. His songs are parables, full of religious realities such as sin, temptation, forgiveness, and hope. His lyrics reflect reverence for life, respect for the dignity of people, and awe at the deep-seated quest for meaning.

Fr. Andrew Greeley, an author, sociologist, and journalist, was a huge fan of Springsteen, saluting him as a "blue-collar prophet and Catholic troubadour." The priest hailed his "Tunnel of Love" album in 1987 as "maybe a more important event in this country than the visit of Pope John Paul II. … Troubadours are always more important than theologians or bishops." For Greeley, Springsteen is a protest singer in two very important ways. He protests against a society that snuffs out dreams and stifles people. He also rails against the human condition and its inevitable anguish.

Springsteen knows what his music means to his fans at his concerts, who identify with his songs and their hurting protagonists, in need of more than what life often delivers. At one show, he roared to the crowd: "I can't promise you life everlasting, but I can promise you life right now." God is never more real than he is at the present moment, even in a loud stadium ruled by a whirling-dervish singer who got out while he was young but knows that the two lanes that can take you anywhere always lead back to where you belong.

DION

Few recording artists have enjoyed the sustained success of Dion. Born in 1939, Dion Francis DiMucci ruled the pop charts in the late 1950s and early 1960s with songs such as "Runaround Sue" and "The Wanderer." In 1968, he tapped into Americans' grief over the assassinations of Martin Luther King Jr. and Robert Kennedy with the lovely, mournful "Abraham, Martin and John." In 2020, his blues album featuring appearances by such luminaries as Bruce Springsteen, Paul Simon, and Van Morrison topped the blues charts.

His faith life is an epic story in itself. Raised Catholic, he stepped away from the Church, battled drug addiction, steadied himself through an Ignatian twelve-step program, became a born-again Christian, and then returned to the Faith of his youth.

Our Lady of Mount Carmel Catholic Church in Little Italy in the Bronx was his boyhood church. His aunts were ardent Catholics, but not his parents. His mother was virtuous but not a churchgoer.

Dion abused drugs, including heroin, from ages fourteen to twenty-eight. After singer Frankie Lymon, a friend, died of an overdose in 1968, Dion was devastated — and terrified he would be next. He dropped to his knees to pray, and he credits God with keeping him sober ever since.

He also credits a twelve-step spiritual program based on Saint Ignatius's Spiritual Exercises. "It's designed to lead you into union with God. And that's a very peaceful place! A place of wisdom, a place of power, of serenity; it's home. I'm home, and I'm not living in a chaotic world, because I'm living in God's presence, or trying to, a day at a time," he told *Catholic World Report* in 2020.

After embracing evangelical Christianity, he returned to Catholicism — for the first time, actually — thanks to a providential sequence of events. By chance, he watched an inspiring episode of *The Journey Home* on EWTN and then visited Mount Carmel in the Bronx. He knew in his heart he had arrived home. Change washed over him.

"Open my brain, you'd see a peaceful and ordered mind," he told the *National Catholic Register* in 2020 at the age of eighty. "When you're living in God's presence, it is a beautiful thing. There is nothing like it — peace of mind. So many people are seeking that, but they won't come to him [God]."

Dion is still making music, but a higher power is at work, too. "It's all a gift. This album, I kept telling my wife, is a gift. He's doing it. Don't get me wrong: I'm part of this, but I felt this is a gift."

JIM PETERIK

As the lead singer for the Ides of March, Jim Peterik rose to fame with the rousing 1970 number-one hit "Vehicle." He also wrote Survivor's "Eye of the Tiger" for *Rocky III*. A typical rocker in many ways, Peterik favors purple hair and flamboyant clothes, even while doing errands and chores at or near his home in a leafy Chicago suburb. He relishes playing his electric guitar loudly and chatters at length about how he loves music and being a musician. He rabidly collects vintage guitars and revels in fast cars.

But his lifestyle is anything but fast. He proudly calls himself a "good

Catholic" who has been married for more than forty years. He is pretty much a teetotaler. He plays benefits for homeless shelters and other good causes.

One of his annual traditions is a Christmas Eve performance with his longtime band, the Ides of March, at Holy Name Cathedral in Chicago. One year, the priest there wove a lyric from "Vehicle" into his homily. "Father Dan [Mayall] actually said, 'Great God in heaven, you know he loves you.' It was hilarious," said Peterik.

Peterik, who grew up in a lower-middle-class Chicago suburb, started a garage band as a high school student. The teenage Peterik wrote "Vehicle" to win back a girlfriend. His ploy worked, and Karen later became his wife.

Peterik has written or co-written songs for 38 Special, Lynyrd Skynyrd, Cheap Trick, Brian Wilson, the Beach Boys, REO Speedwagon, and others. He wrote "Eye of the Tiger" after Sylvester Stallone called him and asked him if he could write a song for his third *Rocky* movie. "Is the pope Catholic?" Peterik replied to Stallone.

The Ides of March has released several Christmas albums in the past few years. "There is something lacking in a lot of current Christmas music. A simple thing called spirituality," he said. "I believe in Jesus, and, of course, Christmas is very much about Jesus."

DON McLEAN

Don McLean's epic, eight-and-a-half-minute "American Pie" stormed up the charts in 1972 and reached number one. As everyone knows, the ballad was inspired by the deaths of Buddy Holly, Ritchie Valens, and J. P. Richardson (the Big Bopper) in a plane crash in 1959. McLean was a thirteen-year-old paperboy in New Rochelle, New York, when he saw the story of the accident in his stack of newspapers.

McLean grew up as a practicing Catholic. He attended Villanova University for a time before earning a degree from Iona College, another Catholic school.

The lyrics of "American Pie" are cryptic. McLean has declined over the years to explain them. A few years ago, on an anniversary of the song, CBS News interviewed him. The reporter was friendly, even fawning, with McLean. But when he asked McLean to explain some of the mysterious lines, the singer smiled and waved him off.

Back in 1972, a Chicago disk jockey at a Top-40 station rigorously analyzed the song and puzzled out how the lyrics charted the 1960s and developments in rock 'n' roll. The song obliquely references the Beatles ("The quartet practiced in the park [Central Park]"), the Rolling Stones ("Jack be nimble, Jack be quick"), and Janis Joplin ("Met a girl who sang the blues / And I asked her for some happy news").

But one stanza stumped the disk jockey: "The three men I admire most / The Father, Son, and the Holy Ghost." McLean couldn't possibly be talking about the Holy Trinity, the radio personality insisted.

Well, yes, he probably was. The sensitive singer-songwriter had crafted an ode to the loss of innocence. His faith was woven into his boyhood. Swirling in him, as he lived through the tumultuous 1960s and witnessed the carefree music of his youth give way to darker impulses, was the memory of what he was taught and how it resonated with him.

McLean's spiritual bent also was part of "Vincent," his moving tribute to Van Gogh, the spiritually tormented Dutch painter. The last stanza of the song is haunting — a beautiful, loving soul not able to endure the harshness of his life.

McLean had an up-and-down career, and his personal life was roiled by two divorces and a domestic-violence incident. But he gaped in wonder at starry nights and mourned the loss of innocence. His was a soul engaged with a world that was troubled but which he loved.

VII

WRITERS

The poet T. S. Eliot said you never meet the same person twice. When you encounter a friend or family member on Tuesday, even if you talked to him on Monday, he is different because his experiences have, if only slightly, altered who he was.

Eliot was exaggerating to make a point — that we change and evolve. As a writer, he knew we can truly change overnight, especially if we have read a powerful book the night before. What can shake and stir the soul like a good book? When we get to the end of a beloved book and reluctantly set it down for the last time, we feel in our heart of hearts we know something priceless and ineffable that we didn't know before, and we've grown as a person and changed for the better.

Writers are Catholic in two ways. They might spin tales about priests and nuns or other characters prone to spiritual musings. Or they might subtly evince their faith by creating a fictional world in which sin and redemption may not be directly addressed but lurk in corners and recesses and hover intangibly over everyday concerns. These writers generate stories informed by a Catholic imagination and a Catholic sensibility. Kafka said, "A book must be an axe for the frozen sea within us." With Catholic writers, the waters that lie beneath the surface run gloriously deep and flow toward the eternal.

Here we'll bypass the prominent Catholic writers such as Flannery O'Connor, Walker Percy, Graham Greene, Alice McDermott, Ron Hansen, and Andre Dubus. There are pleasures and treasures to be found in other writers not typically associated with Catholicism.

WILLIAM SHAKESPEARE

Was the world's greatest writer a secret Catholic?

In Elizabethan England, religion was both pervasive and divisive. Strict laws prohibited religious freedom. Catholics were fined, imprisoned, and even executed for their beliefs. Most scholars maintain that Shakespeare remained loyal to the Church of England. But a few insist that a long trail of circumstantial evidence indicates he was a recusant, someone who refused to accept the authority of that church.

The numerous clues to his Catholicism are tantalizing. Shakespeare's family had substantial Catholic ties. His mother, Mary Arden, belonged to a prominent Catholic family. One family member was executed for hiding a priest. Shakespeare's father, John, was fined for refusing to attend Church of England services. In his father's house, where Will was born, a document related to St. Edmund Campion was discovered hidden in the rafters. Campion had been tortured and killed for spreading Catholicism during the reign of Queen Elizabeth.

Shakespeare was born in 1564, and not much is known about his life in the 1580s, the so-called Lost Years. Some scholars believe he was a tutor to a Catholic family in Lancashire, a stronghold of Catholicism. In any case, mirroring our own age, in which artists tend to be countercultural, the London theater scene was rife with Catholic sensibilities and sympathies. The playwright would have rubbed shoulders daily with actors, writers, and stagehands who chafed under England's repressions.

Shakespeare's plays abound with Catholic references. He was intimately familiar with Catholic rituals and beliefs. Catholics were presented sympathetically. The Franciscan friars, in particular — fiercely suppressed by Henry VIII before Shakespeare emerged as an artist — are part of his oeuvre: there was Friar Laurence in *Romeo and Juliet* and Friar Francis in *Much Ado about Nothing*.

Shakespeare may have been married as a Catholic. He and Anne Hathaway shunned their local church and instead were married in a nearby village by a minister who was later accused of being a Catholic.

Shakespeare's will provides the last piece of evidence of his state of mind. He left nothing to his Protestant family members and nearly everything to his daughter Susanna, suspected of being a Catholic.

Shakespeare remains a cipher in many ways. "Every age creates its own Shakespeare," a Shakespeare scholar declared. For a playwright who captured so much of what it means to be human, it would be strange if he did not incorporate some dimension or degree of Catholicism in his artistic vision and in his soul.

ERNEST HEMINGWAY

Ernest Hemingway was a disillusioned writer among the Lost Generation in Paris, a big-game hunter in untamed Africa, and a living-large bullfighting aficionado in festive Pamplona, Spain. But for all his macho posturing, hard drinking, womanizing, and myriad other manifest faults, Hemingway was a Catholic. He prayed, practiced the Faith, and worried about his soul and the eternal fates of loved ones. His fiction, in which characters seem to flail about in a godless world, grapples with essential Catholic matters such as suffering and redemption.

Hemingway grew up predisposed to religion. His hometown was upper-middle-class Oak Park, bordering Chicago. It was a placid, leafy village drenched in Victorian values. The teamsters who drove the local roads said they knew they were in Oak Park when the saloons stopped and the steeples began. Town elders espoused Calvinist ideals of hard

work, discipline, and good deeds.

Young Ernest grew up in a strongly religious environment. His grandfather led heartfelt prayers before meals, and his father was a devout Protestant who displeased other doctors in town by offering his services for free to the disadvantaged. Ernest (back row, fourth from right) sang in the choir at the First Congregational Church and absorbed weekly sermons from a fiery minister who spoke of a masculine, forceful Christ.

Hemingway worked as a reporter for the *Kansas City Star* when World War I erupted. He volunteered as an ambulance driver for the Red Cross. He was stationed on the Italian front and handing out chocolate to soldiers in a dugout when a mortar blast struck. A soldier next to him was killed instantly. A second, whose legs were blown off, would die shortly after. The eighteen-year-old Hemingway was hit by shrapnel in his right foot, knee, thighs, scalp, and hands.

Severely wounded, he faded in and out of consciousness for hours. Hemingway was given the last rites by a priest chaplain in the Italian army. But he survived.

His next brush with Catholicism was more enduring and consensual. He was a married man in 1925 when he met and fell in love with Pauline Pfeiffer, a writer for Paris *Vogue* and a devout Catholic. Young Pauline had been taught by nuns at a Catholic high school in St. Louis.

Mary Pfeiffer, her mother, was so devout that she refused to move from St. Louis with Pauline to a small town in Arkansas until Paul, her husband, assured her they would be able to get to Sunday Mass. Eventually, her husband converted a downstairs room into a chapel so a local priest could say Mass there.

After converting to Catholicism, Hemingway married Pauline Pfeiffer in 1927. The archbishop of Paris granted the dispensation for the annulment and marriage. Hemingway didn't dabble in the Faith or convert merely because of his marriage. The writer set out to be a practicing Catholic. He went to Mass. He fasted on Fridays. He visited cathedrals and pilgrimage sites in Europe, lit votive candles for the intentions of friends, and wore religious medals. In a letter, he wrote, "If I am anything but a Catholic ... I cannot imagine taking any other religion seriously."

All three of Hemingway's children were brought up Catholic. Thirty years after marrying Pfeiffer, when he won the Nobel Prize in Literature in 1954, he gave his medal as a votive offering to the Virgin of Charity of El Cobre.

Hemingway's commitment to his faith caused problems within his family, owing partly to long-standing resentments. In December 1928, foreshadowing Ernest's own demise, Hemingway's father, beset by depression, shot himself at home in Oak Park. Arriving home and taking charge, roiling his sister, Hemingway told his family he had a Mass said for their father. He also told them his father's soul was in purgatory because of the suicide and they needed to pray fervently for him.

That the public did not identify the celebrated writer with Catholicism was fine with Hemingway. He knew he would be taken less seriously if labeled a Catholic writer. Moreover, although known for his braggadocio and not above fabricating tales of his piety to shocked friends, privately he was insecure about his faith. He wrote to a priest friend, "I have always had more faith than intelligence or knowledge, and I have never wanted to be known as a Catholic writer because I know the importance of setting an example — and I have never set a good example. ... Also I am a very dumb Catholic and I have so much faith that I hate to examine into it."

In the public eye, Hemingway is identified with the Lost Generation, and his writings are considered to be bathed in a secular ethos. Websites dedicated to atheism quote Hemingway. Conservative groups objecting to his novels and their "secular humanism" have managed to remove his books from school curriculums. Yet a number of scholars see Hemingway far differently. His writing reveals a "profound sacramental sense of ritual, pilgrimage and sacrifice," said Matthew Nickel. Hemingway expert H. R. Stoneback agrees: " 'The Sun Also Rises,' far from being the chronicle of the aimless Lost Generation that it is often taken for, is Hemingway's first meditation on the theme of pilgrimage."

Hemingway's writing is so Catholic that he can be compared thematically to Flannery O'Connor, the ultimate Catholic writer of the twentieth century, whose fictional world was undergirded by Catholic theology. The writings of both are steeped in the human condition: suffering and dying. "What we do in the face of that unavoidable reality is their focus," says writer and professor Angela Alaimo O'Donnell. Their fictional universes are suffused with the Catholic themes of suffering, violence, and redemption.

Critics saluted Hemingway's protagonists for their "grace under pressure," an ability to forge ahead in a meaningless, godless world. But his concept of grace can be re-evaluated in understanding the religious sensibility that subtly shades his writing. In his fiction are moments of mysticism and transcendence, deeply Catholic sensations that suggest redemption, says O'Donnell. The bullfighter in *Death in the Afternoon* achieves a rapture "that takes a man out of himself and makes him feel immortal." In centuries past and in other books, men and women found higher meaning, a taste of heaven, through religious ritual or solidarity with others. In Hemingway, an apostle of the outdoors, sport, and masculinity, the arena for spirituality comes in the guise of a bullring.

O'Connor herself recognized a kindred soul in Hemingway. She wrote to her spiritual director, a Jesuit priest:

The Catholic fiction writer has very little high-powered "Catholic" fiction to influence him except that written by [Bloy, Bernanos, Mauriac,] and Greene. But at some point reading them reaches the place of diminishing returns and you get more benefit from reading someone like Hemingway, where there is apparently a hunger for a Catholic completeness in life.

Evelyn Waugh said it more succinctly: Hemingway was "really at heart a Catholic author."

The Catholic impulse was there all along, even before Hemingway converted. In 1925, he released the short story that established his reputation. "Big Two-Hearted River" features Nick Adams, Hemingway's fictional stand-in. Adams returns to his old fishing terrain after the war. He's emotionally battered, desperate for meaning, for redemption.

Critics praised the spare style of this new writer and noted the regenerative power of nature in a world roiled by existential chaos. But Nick is not alone in the woods. When he stops to rest in a pine grove, it's as if he has entered a sacred space, like the churches back in Oak Park, according to writer and professor David King: "The trunks of the trees went straight up or slanted toward each other. ... He looked up at the sky, through the branches, and then shut his eyes. ... There was a wind high up in the branches."

Peace ultimately eluded Hemingway. After his suicide, he was buried under a blanket of red roses. A Catholic priest from Our Lady of the Snows in Ketchum, Idaho, said prayers at his graveside.

Toni Morrison

In *Beloved*, Toni Morrison's 1987 novel that won the Pulitzer Prize, Sethe, a former slave, grapples with the physical, emotional, and spiritual trauma she endured. She carries a "tree on my back" from her whippings. Morrison's characters often carry, if not so literally, a cross. "Black women have held, have been given the cross. They don't walk near it. They're often on it," Morrison said.

Her word choice, the "cross," is intentional. When Morrison died in

2019, she was hailed as the greatest Catholic writer of her time. Her characters wrestle with spiritual struggles. Their faith is woven into who they are. Redemption hovers in the air as the ultimate prize.

The first Black American to win the Nobel Prize in Literature, Morrison wrote eleven novels. She was not just a writer who happened to be a Catholic or a writer whose faith was important to her. Her characters' identities were wrapped up in where they stood before God. Morrison delved deeply into the lives of Blacks, and religion was not incidental to them but was a hallmark of their existence, often the crucible through which they negotiated their difficult journey through a society hostile to them.

Jesuit Fr. Mark Bosco, an expert on Catholic writers, has said that Morrison's novels mined Christianity and the Christian story in America. "In some ways, it's the Christian narrative kind of reworked and investigated and interrogated in the black bodies of her characters," he wrote.

The Black suffering of Morrison's characters recalls the Passion, argues writer Nick Ripatrazone in *Longing for an Absent God*, his exploration of faith in American fiction. "Morrison's theology is one of the Passion: of scarred bodies, public execution and private penance." Morrison's novels, delving into the Black experience in America and its horrific bodily suffering and social degradation, function as a version of an American Passion play.

Morrison's public identity — her name — was a direct consequence of her commitment to Catholicism. Born and raised in Lorain, Ohio, she attended an African Methodist Episcopal Church with her mother. "Everybody read the Bible," she said of the congregants. Some of her extended family members, including a cousin dear to her, were Catholic.

In 1943, as a twelve-year-old, Chloe Wofford (her name then) converted to Catholicism.

Her confirmation name was Anthony, after St. Anthony of Padua. Anthony became her middle name, and her family shortened that to Toni. Her last name changed after she married Harold Morrison.

She said was drawn to Catholicism because of "its aesthetics. That's shallow, I understand. But that's what it was, until I grew a little older and began to take it seriously and then took it seriously for years and years and years."

Religion was impossible for her to ignore in conveying Black lives. In her essay "God's Language," she noted that surveys at the time showed that 96 percent of Blacks believed in God. "The history of African Americans that narrows or dismisses religion in both their collective and individual life, in their political and aesthetic activity, is more than incomplete — it may be fraudulent. Therefore, among the difficulties before me is the daunting one of showing not just how their civic and economic impulses respond to their religious principles, but how their everyday lives were inextricably bound with these principles."

Religious impulses animate Morrison's characters. In crafting imaginary worlds, she could not put God in a box and escort him from the premises without betraying what was true to her characters. Her writing is "about love or its absence," she said. Its power and heft derive from its grounding in fundamental longings. "What saved me was knowing that I was going to take religion seriously, I mean belief," she wrote.

Later in life, Morrison moved away from formal worship. But Catholicism remained alluring. "I might easily be seduced to go back to church because I like the controversy as well as the beauty of this particular Pope Francis," she told National Public Radio's Terry Gross in 2015. "He's very interesting to me."

JACK KEROUAC

On the Road will likely still be read a century from now. It epitomized the beat culture of the 1950s, and after its publication in 1957, Jack Kerouac was anointed as the spokesperson for the Beat Generation.

His literary talent blossomed, despite a lascivious, scandalous lifestyle. He was promiscuous, misogynistic, racist, and anti-Semitic. He alienated family and friends and drank himself to death at only forty-seven years.

Yet he was a soul in search of meaning, in search of God. Personal virtues, or the lack of them, and spirituality are not mutually exclusive. When Kerouac was laid in his casket in 1969 at St. Jean Baptiste Church in Lowell, Massachusetts, family and friends did not object to what the mortician did: draped a rosary over his folded hands.

For Kerouac, literature was a stab in the dark at the divine. "All I write about is Jesus," he told the *Paris Review*. His one masterpiece was "really a story about two Catholic buddies roaming the country in search of God." On *Firing Line*, he told fellow Catholic William F. Buckley Jr. that, as a Catholic, he believed in "order, tenderness, and piety."

Kerouac was raised in New England by devout parents who had moved to that area from French Canada. Kerouac's father wore around his neck a rosary blessed by Trappist monks. Young Jack attended Catholic schools and served as an altar boy. A kind priest at St. Jean Baptiste Church nudged the teenage Jack toward his literary destiny.

"Everybody is laughing at me," Kerouac told Fr. Armand "Spike" Morissette.

"Why?"

"Because I want to be a writer."

"I'm not laughing."

"You're not?"

"No, I think it's wonderful."

"Well, I'll be a writer. I'll write a lot of books."

"More power to you. It's possible. Writers are people like us. But let me warn you. You're in for a lot of disappointment."

"I don't mind."

"Then congratulations. I'll be helping you, if I can. Writers can be very important. They can influence countless people."

Kerouac was not a Mass-goer as an adult. He explored Buddhism and Eastern spirituality. But his Catholicism clung to him like a wet shirt. He often stepped inside Catholic churches to kneel and pray. He remembered and treasured the brief Marian prayers of his youth and retained a special fondness for the "Little Way" of Saint Thérèse.

His world-weary friends teased him about his Catholicism. He defended the Church to them.

On the Road was a celebration of unbridled freedom. It also was a testament to the desire for a higher purpose, for authenticity, and to a turning away from the shallow and the phony. Near the beginning of the book he writes, "The only people for me are the mad ones, the ones who are mad to live, mad to talk, mad to be saved."

When he was in his early thirties, during a visit to the church of his youth, Kerouac grasped what his quest was all about. Kneeling alone in silence, "I suddenly realized, Beat means Beatitude! Beatific!" He later further explained, "Because I am Beat, I believe in Beatitude and that God so loved the world He gave His only begotten son to it."

Kerouac failed to transform that belief into a life of piety and virtue. Celebrating his funeral Mass, Father Morissette chose to focus on his grappling toward God. He linked the troubled writer's life to the Gospel passage about Emmaus (involving two disciples who encountered the risen Jesus on a road but failed to realize it was he): "Wasn't it like a fire burning in us when he [Kerouac] talked to us on the road?" (see Lk 24:32).

MARY HIGGINS CLARK

The Queen of Suspense wrote fifty-six novels and sold more than a hundred million books in the United States alone. Mary Higgins Clark, who died in 2020 at age ninety-two, churned out page-turners that gradually lifted veils of secrecy and cunning. Few of her readers realized how she turned the page on her own struggles earlier in her life and how her faith bolstered her. "Her own life taught her lessons of resilience, strengthened by her Catholic faith, that she shared with her fictional heroines," read her obituary in the *Los Angeles Times*.

In 1956, when she was twenty-eight, Clark sold her first story for one hundred dollars to the Catholic magazine *Extension*. This was after a dozen years of rejections from publishers. She had three children at the time. She became exponentially busier six years later when her husband died of a heart attack, leaving her with their five children.

Clark didn't give up writing. She rose before dawn to write from five o'clock to seven o'clock, while her children slept, and then carpooled to Manhattan to work at an advertising agency. Her first novel was finally published in 1969.

Her books reflect her own difficulties. Her typical protagonist is a strong, courageous, Catholic heroine who triumphs over violence, intrigue, or adversity. "Her faith will help her persevere," Clark told Catholic News Service. Clark herself was deeply involved with Catholic institutions. She attended Catholic schools as a youth in New York. She served as a trustee both of Fordham University, where she studied philosophy, and Providence College in Rhode Island.

Priests, churches, and Catholic schools are often part of her stories. Clark once incorporated her pastor at her church in Saddle River, New Jersey, into one of her books, *I've Got My Eyes on You*. A writing instructor years ago told her, "Write what you know," she recounts. "I'd grown up observing examples of Catholic women who were strong figures and persevered against difficult odds. It was natural to model my characters after the people I knew."

Miracles also play a role in some stories. *The Shadow of Your Smile* revolves around a murder and an ancient church manuscript. A character in the book, Dr. Monica Callaghan, marvels at the faith of an anguished mother as her young son, Michael, appears to overcome terminal cancer. "I cannot understand why I was so resistant to the idea that the power of prayer was the cause of Michael's return to health," says Dr. Callaghan. "I was a witness to the absolute act of faith of his mother when I told her he was terminally ill. It was arrogant of me to be so dismissive of her faith, especially since the proof of it is her eight-year-old healthy little boy."

Clark's books eschew profanity. They end happily, and the main characters are upright. The Church is portrayed positively, as a place of solace and comfort. Clark joked about her favorable attitude toward Catholicism. "I don't recall if I've ever created a character that was Catholic and a villain," she said. "If I did, I hope I portrayed him or her as a fallen-away Catholic."

SIR ARTHUR CONAN DOYLE

Arthur Conan Doyle was born in 1859 in Scotland into a staunchly Catholic Irish family. His immortal sleuth, Sherlock Holmes, was relentlessly observant and intelligent. Doyle was no mental slouch either. He was a medical doctor as well as a writer. Jesuit schooling, though Doyle loathed its rigor and harshness, formed his intellect and prepared him to think logically and independently.

Doyle attended Hodder House, a Jesuit prep school, as a lad and then Stonyhurst Boarding College, founded in 1593, in England. His doting uncle Conan wrote to his parents that the school "in mere secular education, from experience and their employment therein, of the highest order of the mind, is unmatched."

His family brooked no deviation from Catholic orthodoxy. Doyle's uncle Dick, normally easygoing, refused to pitch his illustrations to *Punch* magazine after it ridiculed the pope. But Doyle became an ag-

nostic as a young adult, and this led to a rupture with his family.

Doyle eventually turned to spiritualism. He frequented séances and believed it was possible to communicate with the dead, though he broke with many spiritualists for advocating following the moral example of Jesus.

Doyle was a perplexing figure. He defended the Boer War, in which he served as a volunteer doctor. The British were accused of atrocities during the war in Africa, yet he roundly condemned the Belgian horrors in the Congo.

Doyle's rejection of Catholicism, sadly, mirrored the path of many Catholics who forge their own spiritual paths as adults. Yet he continued as an avid spiritual seeker, utterly determined to see beyond the here and now and reach for the eternal.

VIII

MOVIES AND TELEVISION

In *The Moviegoer*, the 1961 debut novel by Catholic writer Walker Percy, Jack "Binx" Bolling, a young stockbroker, struggles with his family relationships and grapples with trauma from his experiences in the Korean War. He finds more meaning in movies than he does in his own troubled life.

Movies are powerful. In the darkened theater, we lose a sense of self and, for two hours or so, enter into another world. Art directs us outward, away from petty routines and toward a comprehension of reality not bogged down by our narrow, self-centered consciousness. Film critic Roger Ebert, who attended Catholic grade school in central Illinois and credited nuns for shining a light for him on societal ills, called movies "empathy machines." They make us better people by helping us understand human nature and identifying with others.

Movies and television crack open a door on the lives of others and dare us not only to take a peek but also to be influenced and changed by what we see. It's God who crouches behind that door. "The world is charged with the grandeur of God," wrote the Jesuit poet Gerard Manley Hopkins. Films that have nothing overtly to do with religion can deliver a spiritual experience. The sacred is in the soil, in the air, in others, and in works of art such as films.

More so than members of other faiths, Catholics are ripe for making films charged with meaning and watching them with a heightened sensitivity to that meaning. Catholic churches are dramatic, visual places filled with stained-glass windows, statues, and paintings. Our religious rituals, the way we celebrate the Mass and the sacraments, are steeped in a colorful spiritual choreography. Our liturgies are powerful, multisensory experiences with music, incense, flowers, candles, holy water, and vestments. The Catholic imagination finds a natural home in film, wrote Jesuit Richard Blake, a film history professor.

Movies and TV are rife with Catholic actors, directors, and themes. Hollywood may be crass and immoral on occasion, but it's not Babylon. It's us.

JOHN WAYNE

Was there ever a man on the silver screen more virile, tougher, or more confident and capable than John Wayne? He always won, mostly with his fists or a six-shooter. Then he rode off on his horse with the girl. The Duke was larger than life, seemingly impervious to the stings and lashes of ordinary mortals.

Yet there lay Wayne in June 1972 at the UCLA Medical Center. He was only seventy-two and, before this second terrible bout with cancer, was still robust, still full of vigor and brimstone. Now even talking was difficult.

Wayne was not a regular church-goer. Outspoken in standing up for conservative values, he lived by his conscience, not by precepts spoken by ministers from pulpits. His first wife, Josephine, was Catholic. She raised their children Catholic. Wayne pestered his kids to listen to their mother. "Have you gone to church?" he often asked. His son Michael remembered that nagging: "He was like an old woman that way."

His daughter Josephine prayed regularly for his conversion. Wayne sometimes joined the family for Mass on Christmas, Easter, and an occasional Sunday.

The film industry was not especially conducive to piety and practicing a faith. Still, a few titans of Hollywood surprisingly clung to their faith. Director John Ford, who made classics such as *Stagecoach*, *The Searchers*, and *The Quiet Man* with Wayne, brought priests to remote locations and required the cast and crew to attend Mass. Wayne was known to drop a wad of bills in the collection basket. He respected priests and befriended several.

Priests repaid that respect. Wayne's basic integrity, which his films drew out and amplified, was appealing. His battle with cancer was well known, and one day a bishop from Panama, a big film buff who was visiting Los Angeles, went to the hospital on a whim and asked to see Wayne. The bishop spent fifteen minutes with the actor.

The bishop told Michael, "Your father's in good shape. Don't worry about him." Michael knew he was dying and understood that the prelate was referring to his spiritual health.

Their dad was famously stubborn and resisted being told what to do, so his kids knew they had to be strategic in talking to him about the most profound matters. Michael's brother Patrick hatched a plan. "Father Curtis, the hospital chaplain, called. Would you like to see him, dad?"

Actually, Patrick had called the priest.

Wayne had been drifting in and out of consciousness. But he heard Patrick. "Yeah," he mumbled before drifting off.

Wayne revived when Father Curtis approached his bed. "That was a small miracle," recalled Michael. Wayne found the strength to extend his hand to the priest. "Hi, Father. How are you?"

The priest baptized Wayne and gave him the sacraments. Wayne quickly nodded off and never regained consciousness. He died the next day. "We felt a tremendous loss," said Michael. "But it was tempered with the tremendous joy of knowing we had been instrumental in bringing him together with God in the final moments of his life."

GRACE KELLY

A major star in 1954, the glamorous Grace Kelly won an Oscar that year for best actress in *The Country Girl*. Her career arrow was still pointing up, way up. That year, she worked with Alfred Hitchcock and Jimmy Stewart in *Rear Window* and *Dial M for Murder* and with Cary Grant in *To Catch a Thief*.

In Monaco that same year, Prince Rainier was eager to catch a bride. A committed Catholic, the prince turned to his chaplain and adviser, Fr. Francis Tucker. Out of the blue, the priest suggested that the lovely actress Grace Kelly might be "the one." Rainier watched her movies and "was smitten." He and the companionable "Father Tuck" drove

off to Lourdes to pray for guidance.

Not long afterward, as fate would have it, Kelly went to the Riviera to film *To Catch a Thief.* Father Tuck invited her to Monaco, she met the prince, and the two walked the grounds for a while. A written correspondence followed. They were devoted pen pals before they even held hands.

One thing they had in common was a dedication to their Catholic faith. Born in Philadelphia in 1929 in an affluent family, Kelly attended Ravenhill Academy, run by the Religious of the Assumption, a teaching order of sisters. "They were remarkable women and I was enormously fond of them," Kelly told her biographer Donald Spoto. "They were strict about our studies, but also very, very kind. However rigorous their religious life, the nuns understood young girls and devoted themselves completely to our educational and spiritual welfare."

Kelly attended Mass even while filming. Renowned designer Oleg Cassini, who was smitten with her, followed her to France in 1954. She shook off his romantic advances and instead took him to Mass with her.

Kelly had grown disenchanted with Hollywood even as her fame rocketed:

I think I really hated Hollywood without knowing it. I had lots of acquaintances there, and people I enjoyed working with and learned a lot from. But I found a great deal of fear among people in Hollywood — fear of not succeeding, and fear of succeeding but then losing the success. I've often said it was a pitiable place, full of insecure people who had crippling problems. The unhappiness out there was like smog — it covered everything.

After she won the Oscar, she trudged back to her hotel suite with the statue. She felt empty. She wanted to get married and have children. That evening, which for most people would have been triumphant and joyous, was "the loneliest moment of my life," she admitted.

Rainier, who believed that his prayers in France had been answered, soon proposed to Kelly. When Father Tuck later told her about the prince's trip to Lourdes, she was astonished. Her confirmation name happened to be Bernadette.

The Prince and Miss Kelly married in 1956. It was perhaps the most famous wedding of the twentieth century, watched on live TV by thirty million viewers.

Kelly happily retired from acting at age twenty-six. She and the prince had three children, whom she doted on. Instead of using a nanny, she looked after the children herself.

She was done with Hollywood but not quite with filming. In the early 1980s she did three short film projects for Family Theater, founded by Fr. Patrick Peyton, "the Rosary Priest," whose signature phrase was, "The family that prays together stays together."

Legendary director John Huston hosted the first film, in which Princess Grace prays the Rosary with Peyton. She also filmed *Seven Last Words*, a Lenten reflection. In 1981, she traveled to the Vatican to record *The Nativity*. Cary Grant's voice also was used for the film. (The films can be viewed on the Family Theater website.)

Family Theater's gratitude to Kelly continues to this day. Outside its office in Los Angeles is a parking spot labeled "P. Grace."

In 1982, Kelly had a stroke while driving. She never recovered consciousness and died on September 14, the feast of the Triumph of the Cross. She was fifty-two.

GREGORY PECK

Gregory Peck is remembered for his larger-than-life screen roles. He portrayed the fiery Captain Ahab in *Moby Dick*, the manly fighter pilot in *Twelve O'Clock High*, and, of course, Atticus Finch, the heroic lawyer and loving father in *To Kill a Mockingbird*. A highly skilled actor, he was able to lose himself in a character.

The real Peck off-screen knew who he was: a Catholic committed to his faith and to good works. He was awarded the Presidential Medal of Freedom for his humanitarian efforts. Peck had his own measurements of value, not connected to celebrity or stardom. He described Pope John Paul II as the most impressive man he ever met. The pope would have none of it. "God bless you, Gregory. God bless you in your mission," the pontiff told the actor.

Eldred Gregory Peck was born in 1916, in La Jolla, California, to a father who was Catholic and a mother who converted after marriage. His father's family hailed from Ireland, and relatives there resisted the English authorities. Peck was related to Thomas Ashe, who participated in the Easter Rising and died while being force-fed during a hunger strike in 1917.

When he was ten, Peck's parents placed him in a Catholic military school, St. John's Military Academy in Los Angeles. "Maybe they decided I was having too much fun in La Jolla," he said. "Or that I needed discipline." He got plenty of that at the Catholic school. The students prayed before and after meals, before and after class, and before bedtime. "From the time we woke up until the time we went to bed, they had us hemmed in," Peck joked.

But he credited the school with forming his character. "One of the things that you didn't do there was quit anything you started. You went to the finish," he said.

His second film, in 1943, was *The Keys of the Kingdom*, in which he played a self-sacrificing missionary priest in China. Peck received an Oscar nomination for best actor. He had a little help preparing for the role: He consulted with a Jesuit missionary to China. Peck remained friends with Fr. Albert O'Hara and generously supported his work.

Forty years later, Peck made another Catholic film: *The Scarlet and the Black,* based on a true story from World War II. Peck played Msgr. Hugh O'Flaherty, who hides thousands of escaped POWs in occupied Rome.

When Peck first read the script for *To Kill a Mockingbird* in 1961, he knew the role of Atticus was a rare opportunity. "God was smiling on me," he said. Peck had shown an ability as an actor to convey decency and probity. He upped his game in the film. In the character Atticus, Peck, his acting capabilities, and the scripted role all came together. As Harper Lee, the author of *To Kill a Mockingbird*, said, "In that film, the man and the part met."

Peck died in 2003. Cardinal Roger Mahony of Los Angeles held a public service for the beloved actor after a small, private funeral. "He lived his life authentically, as God called and willed him and placed him in this world, with gifts and talents," the cardinal said.

ALFRED HITCHCOCK

"The Master of Suspense," Alfred Hitchcock, was also a practicing Catholic whose films were not overly religious but often explored themes closely related to his faith.

Jesuits in London educated the future director. Biographers attribute the discipline and order of his filmmaking to his rigorous education.

His faith remained a ballast in his life. On his first trip to Paris in the 1920s, as a young man, instead of availing himself of the delights of the city, Hitchcock rushed to Mass. As a successful director, he attended weekly Mass at Good Shepherd Church in Hollywood. Gazing at the nouveau riche in the pews, employing his droll humor, he opined that his church ought to be called "Our Lady of the Cadillacs."

His films are rich, often subtly, with Catholic imagery. There is the church bell tower in *Vertigo*, a plaster cast of a woman's praying hands in *Psycho*, a "nun" in high heels in *The Lady Vanishes*, and, in his last film, *Family Plot*, the kidnapping of a bishop.

His one explicitly Catholic film was *I Confess*, a drama about a priest who learns during confession that a handyman at the parish has murdered someone. The priest himself then becomes the prime suspect. Hitchcock shows a resolute Father] Logan walking the streets of Quebec and passing statues of Christ carrying the Cross atop the city's churches. The priest cannot divulge what he knows. He won't divulge it. He will not let the cup pass.

The innocent man falsely accused is a standard Hitchcock theme, an obsession that sprang, as film buffs know, from his terrifying experience of being locked up in jail as a boy. The heroes of *The Thirty-Nine Steps* and *Young and Innocent* are wrongly suspected of murder and forced to flee. In the classic *North by Northwest*, Cary Grant's character is similarly mistaken for someone else and is chased across the country.

These are plots. But as critics have pointed out, Hitchcock's movies are also stories of the Passion, an innocent suffering for others. Guilt and innocence are in some ways less important in his films than the manner in which a protagonist responds to his misfortune.

Hitchcock was not a choirboy, nor do his films shy away from the dark side of the soul. But in his films are torment, struggle, and the highest stakes. The resolutions in his films leave us with grand conclusions. When there is a happy ending, "our quest to redeem time and recover innocence" is affirmed, said critic Lesley Brill. When they end tragically, Brill said, "Hitchcock, like most of us, must have fervently hoped that rebirth in love should be the way of things, and dreaded that it might not be."

In real life, as he aged and declined, Hitchcock tried to counter the dread of dying by drawing closer to his faith. A Jesuit priest said Mass regularly at his home. During his last days, whenever he received Holy Communion, he wept.

GEORGE COHAN

Say the name George Cohan, and most Americans of a certain age think of film actor James Cagney whipsawing across the stage to the strutting tones of "Yankee Doodle Dandy." Genuinely born on the Fourth of July, the hyperpatriotic Cohan was the ultimate American. He helped create America, or at least one of its iconic art forms — the musical comedy, the staple of Broadway.

Cohan had his fingerprints all over American culture for decades. During World War I, his song "Over There" was by far the most inspirational and popular American patriotic anthem of the era.

Born in Providence, Rhode Island, in 1879, Cohan was the grandson of immigrants from County Cork. The family name evolved from O'Caomhan to Keohane to Cohan. His father, Jerry, served as a surgeon's orderly in the Civil War and as a harness maker and then was a vaudevillian. George joined the family act as a young boy.

Cohan wrote more than fifty shows and published more than three hundred songs. "Over There" became so synonymous with the war effort that a ship was named *Costigan* after Cohan's grandfather, and the song was played during the christening. Other Cohan songs that became standards were "Give My Regards to Broadway," "The Yankee Doodle Boy," and "You're a Grand Old Flag."

Cohan was exuberantly upfront about his patriotism. During his shows, he often waved the American flag as a finale, which brought down the house.

Given his affection for his country, it was probably not a coincidence that he loved baseball. From casts and crews on Broadway he organized sandlot games, and he asked every actor auditioning for a show of his if he played baseball.

Cohan attended Mass at St. Malachy Chapel, near Broadway. Known as the Actor's Chapel, it held a 4:00 a.m. Mass to accommodate theater folks. Also worshipping there were Rudolph Valentino, Spencer Tracy, Irene Dunne, and Bob Hope. Cohan donated the altar rail at St. Malachy and served as president of the Catholic Actors Guild.

He dearly loved his father, his mentor and "best pal," and his father's death in 1917 devastated Cohan. Years later, when on stage, Cohan would see his father in the wings, smiling at him. He was convinced that what he saw was something more than his imagination at work.

Cohan died in 1942, and his funeral was held at St. Patrick's Cathedral. For the first time in the church's long history, a secular song was played on its great organ. After the Mass, as his casket was borne down the aisle, the cathedral organist, slowly and softly, in a funeral march tempo, played "Over There." Cohan left his audience — for the final time — in tears.

BILL MURRAY

Bill Murray first became famous for his droll, anarchic comic sketches on *Saturday Night Live*. He later starred in enormously successful comedies such as *Stripes* and *Groundhog Day*. He's kind of a class clown unleashed on the rest of us. He's the unnoticed child from a large, loud family, eager to squeeze in a joke or two.

Indeed, Murray is the middle child of nine in a raucous Irish Catholic family. Their home was across the street from their Catholic church in a Chicago suburb, and the Murrays trooped together like a row of ducks to their Catholic school.

Bill's older sister Nancy became a Dominican sister. The stage bug hit her too. She once did a polished, popular, long-running one-woman show about St. Catherine of Siena. The ample revenues went to her congregation. Seeing the show for the first time, brother Bill, not one to lavish praise on a sibling, succinctly told Nancy, "I'd cut fifteen minutes."

The Murrays as a brood eschewed convention and niceties. Not long after Nancy entered the convent, several of her brothers congregated outside the convent windows. "NANCY!" Billy bellowed, according to the *Chicago Tribune*. "We have a bag packed! You can leave! Come on. We'll drive away! We'll take off! NANCY!"

Ultimately, Bill and his brothers were supportive and encouraging. If Catholic school taught Bill anything, it was to do the right thing. The brothers called Nancy at the convent. "They said, 'Stay where you are,'" Nancy recalled. "They told me not to send any more of those pious letters I was writing. Still, they said stay. 'But only stay if you remain our Nancy. We don't want a nun in the family we're embarrassed of.'"

Bill now refers to his sister as "the white sheep of the family." After seeing her show, he told her he bought a DVD of it. "That's for canonization purposes," he told her.

For her part, Sister Nancy treats her brother more conventionally. She likes his movies. Her ministry often may be quite traditional, but his is celluloid. Her review of his 1988 film *Scrooged*: "The message was heartfelt. At the time, I was doing work with the homeless and working in food pantries. I was working out of St. Sylvester Parish [in Chicago]. That movie just kind of brought it all home."

Murray is not the kind of person to wax eloquently or even too fondly on his faith. He plays it for laughs. Asked once what saint appealed to him, he mentioned Pope John XXIII. "I'll buy that one. He's my guy; an extraordinary joyous Florentine who changed the order," he said. "I'm not sure all those changes were right. I tend to disagree with what they call the new mass. I think we lost something by losing the Latin." The sainthood causes of John Paul II and Mother Teresa were to aid the Church and fill pews, he flippantly added. "I think they're [Church leaders] just trying to get current and hot," Murray said.

Murray's humor is grounded in a Catholic sensibility. He has a sunnier view of the world than many comics do. His jokes do not arise from anger and disgust. The world is out of joint and disordered, but for him, the disarray is more comic than tragic. On the big screen, he winks at the world. He is not only amusing but amused.

In recent years, Murray has gained attention for randomly inserting himself into the lives of strangers. He shows up unannounced at weddings of strangers, joins karaoke singers at bars, reads poetry to construction workers, and hops behind the wheel of a cab and, when he learns the cabbie is a musician, tells him to go ahead and play his sax in the back seat.

Being alert and alive is part of being a person of faith. Murray is a court jester and a holy fool, flouting convention and reaching for connection with others. Meeting strangers and spreading surprise and joy are kind of a comic's way of being an itinerant Franciscan friar. "I'm trying to wake that person up. Wake me the hell up," Murray said of his stunts.

THE NUN WHO KISSED ELVIS

In 1957, Dolores Hart was an eighteen-year-old Hollywood beauty when she starred opposite Elvis in *Loving You*. Three years later, she appeared in the teenage classic *Where the Boys Are*. In a mere six years, hailed as the next Grace Kelly, she made eleven films.

In 1963, however, she shocked Hollywood. An MGM limousine dropped her off at the Abbey of Regina Laudis in Bethlehem, Connecticut. Since then, she has lived a contemplative life as a Benedictine nun. Mother Dolores, as she became, has spent the rest of her days devoted to prayer, charity, and manual labor.

She turned her back on fame, money, and even love. In 1962, she had been engaged to Don Robinson, a kind, gentle man who owned a moving company.

How could you give up the glamour of Hollywood?

"How could I not?" she told an interviewer decades ago.

She has been at peace with her decision. "Here I learned to love and live in relationship, and to possess love inclusively. And if you learn to do that, you know the spirit of God."

An only child, she was not raised Catholic. "It was a million-to-one-shot I would ever be a nun," she said.

A friend had first taken her to the abbey in 1957. Something was  gnawing at her soul. She felt a seismic shift in her after appearing in *Lisa*, which dealt with the Holocaust and gruesome experiments done on prisoners at Auschwitz. The frothy world of Hollywood was no match for the tranquility and deep meaning of the abbey.

The former star wears a full-length black habit, rises at 2:00 a.m. to chant prayers in Latin, and cooks, cleans, and tends to farm animals. She has not retreated into an implacable silence. She has given interviews to *People, Good Housekeeping*, and other media outlets. In the late 1990s, she sang on her abbey's *Women in Chant*, a CD of Gregorian chants that reached number forty-five on the Billboard charts. In 2011, she consented to appear in *God Is the Bigger Than Elvis*, a touching 2011 documentary film about her that was nominated for an Oscar.

Being a nun has not been about giving something up. It has made Dolores Hart more herself. Her sense of humor remains intact and sharp. Asked what it was like to kiss Elvis, she tackles the query head-on. "I think the limit for a screen kiss back then was something like 15 seconds. This one has lasted 60 years."

FILMS HONORED BY THE VATICAN

The Vatican keeps busy running the affairs of the Church and attending to the needs of the faithful worldwide. As a sovereign state, it mints its own euros, prints its own stamps, issues passports and license plates, and operates media outlets. It also has its favorite films.

In 1995, in observance of the hundredth anniversary of cinema, the Pontifical Council for Social Communications singled out forty-five movies for their artistic or religious merit.

Perhaps surprisingly, well-regarded Church-related films such as *The Ten Commandments* and *The Bells of St. Mary's* did not make the cut. Instead, many of the films depict characters confronting moral issues.

Among the U.S. films honored were *Stagecoach, Citizen Kane, Modern Times, A Man for All Seasons*, and *On the Waterfront*.

Foreign films included *Chariots of Fire* (Britain), *Gandhi* (Britain), *The Seventh Seal* (Sweden), *Grand Illusion* (France), *Nosferatu* (Germany), and *Dekalog* (Poland).

Films with religious themes included *A Man for All Seasons, Ben Hur, The Passion of Joan of Arc* (France), *Andrei Rublev* (Soviet Union), *Babette's Feast* (Denmark), and *The Mission* (Britain).

In celebrating the films, the Church indirectly distanced herself from her defunct finger-wagging Legion of Decency, which rated some films as "morally objectionable." Three Italian films once given that rating made the new list: *Open City, La Strada*, and *The Bicycle Thief*. In a genuine plot twist, the Church that once reflexively recoiled at movies that dealt with gritty social themes changed course and valued artistry over dull conformity.

Churches on Film

Years ago, actress Ethel Barrymore offered a memorable, cynical take on Hollywood: "The place is unreal. The people are unreal. The flowers are unreal — they don't smell." But the churches in and near Hollywood are real. When a script calls for a Catholic church or just a generically beautiful church, filmmakers often avail themselves of a local sanctuary down the street or at least in California.

Built in 1927 in Gothic Revival style, St. Brendan in Los Angeles is an architectural gem. Its beautiful interior and exterior have made it a favorite of movie and TV producers. Its most notable appearance was in *The War of the Worlds* in 1953. As aliens obliterate the city, terrified Angelenos rush inside St. Brendan's to pray for a miracle.

Other movie appearances included *Armageddon* in 1998, which starred Ben Affleck and Liv Tyler, and *Spider Man 3* in 2007. TV shows filmed here include *The Fugitive, Castle, The Mod Squad, Falcon Quest, Beverly Hills 90210, CSI Miami, Columbo,* and *Murder, She Wrote.*

Situated on Sunset Boulevard, Blessed Sacrament Church in Hollywood is an Italian-Renaissance masterpiece. Dedicated in 1928, it was notable more for its close relationship with Hollywood power brokers than as a filming location. The pastor in the 1920s served as a technical adviser to movies with a religious angle, and parishioners were used as extras. In 1926, when the parish needed money for a new church, Hollywood reciprocated. The studios provided actors and equipment for theatrical shows and festivals. For years, the shows were head and shoulders above a typical parish production.

Actors and directors found a spiritual home at Blessed Sacrament. They were so ubiquitous that the precursor to the Writers and Screen Actors Guilds was formed there. Celebrity weddings and funerals were commonplace at the church. Bing Crosby was married there. John Ford was buried there. Ford's funeral packed the church with a who's who of Hollywood: John Wayne, James Stewart, Charlton Heston, Henry Fonda, Frank Capra, William Wyler, Pat O'Brien, Loretta Young, and Cesar Romero. Ford had been a regular at the church and donated its bronze doors.

The momentous occasions at Blessed Sacrament often revealed that celebrities and their families were not so different from you and me. At her wedding, John Wayne's daughter Melinda Ann teetered while kneeling in front of the altar. The Duke sprang from his pew and caught her before she fell.

St. Monica in Santa Monica became the quintessential Catholic church when it was used in 1944 for *Going My Way*, starring Bing Crosby. The church was an apt choice. The film's director, Leo McCarey, attended the church and was a friend of a former pastor, Msgr. Nicholas Conneally. Crosby's character was based on the monsignor.

Mission Dolores in San Francisco, the city's oldest structure, was used in *Vertigo*, Hitchcock's 1958 classic. In the film, Jimmy Stewart follows Kim Novak to the Mission Dolores cemetery, where her character visits the grave of Carlotta Valdes. The film crew somehow forgot to remove Carlotta's gravestone after filming was completed, and it became a popular tourist attraction until the Mission staff decided the fake stone wasn't appropriate and removed it. In 1968, the church interior was the backdrop for the Henry Fonda–Lucille Ball wedding scene in *Yours, Mine and Ours*.

LILIES OF THE FIELD

In the heartwarming 1963 film *Lilies of the Field*, Sidney Poitier played Homer Smith, an upright Black man who builds a chapel for struggling German nuns. He even finds time to teach them to sing rousing choruses of "Amen." The plot was fictional. But the book by novelist William Barrett that launched the film was based on a real convent in Boulder, Colorado.

The Abbey of St. Walburga began when three nuns fled Nazi oppression in Bavaria in the 1930s and found a home in the wilds of Colorado. They eventually sent for more of their sick and half-starved Benedictine sisters. The indefatigable nuns converted a treeless prairie into a pleasant, though spare, home. They planted hundreds of tiny shade trees and fashioned a chapel out of a run-down barn.

Alas, the nuns were able to escape Hitler but not urban sprawl. A busy highway and subdivisions surrounded their once isolated convent. So in 1997, thanks to land donated by a Denver businessman and his wife, the nuns relocated to a much quieter spot in Virginia Dale, Colorado.

The area is isolated enough for mountain lions to roam here, and a few years ago one snatched a llama guarding the nun's prized cattle. That's right, the nuns transitioned from farmers to ranchers. They raise eighty grass-fed beef cattle. Their herd consists of Galloways and Black Baldies, sometimes crossed with Black Angus.

The steers and heifers meet their Maker after two years. The beef has a long line of regular customers, so buying it is not easy. It's occasionally available in the gift shop.

The nuns' 250 acres also include dogs, cats, pigs, chickens, and goats, which yield artisan cheese. That's not all. A small carpentry shop allows nuns to make a dozen or so coffins a year.

The nuns still wear traditional habits, unless they are doing ranching work. So, because they pray seven times a day, they routinely change from jeans to habits and from habits to jeans.

The abbey hosts retreatants. The simple but satisfying moments enjoyed here leave many visitors in a mood to sing out, "Amen."

THE SCHOOL BUILT BY A MOVIE

Only one school in the country has been built by a movie. That's Sacred Heart School in Southaven, Mississippi.

The Sacred Heart League, based in Walls, Mississippi, hatched the unprecedented project, which took nearly a quarter century to come to fruition. For decades, the league ran missions, schools, and clinics in northern Mississippi, where Catholics represented only 2 percent of the population. The league's priests, sisters, and laity offered the rituals, devotions, and teachings of the Church to Catholics and extended to the needy a wide variety of social services.

The league arrived in Mississippi in 1942. Fr. Leo Dehon, who sought to alleviate the ills of the industrial age, had founded the Congregation of the Sacred Heart in 1878 in France.

The Sacred Heart League raised its outreach funds from the sale of plastic statues of Jesus for car dashboards. "Drive carefully and prayfully" was the catchy motto of the league, begun in 1955. But religious sensibilities changed in the 1960s after Vatican II. Tiny Jesus statues lost their appeal. The league turned to direct-mail solicitations to fund its activities.

By the mid-1970s, that revenue stream also declined. Rising postage rates and increased competition for charitable dollars were to blame. At the same time, the league undertook a self-assessment, analyzing its mission. League officials concluded they were primarily religious communicators, bringing the Good News to society. That mission was borne out by its extensive catalog of religious books and videos. The league also promoted the Faith by sending devotional materials, free of charge, to hospitals, prisons, homes for the elderly, the military, and religious-education programs.

The league hit upon a novel way both to raise funds and spread gospel values: to make movies. "Film is the most powerful medium in the world," Roger Courts, the league's director, said then. "Hollywood films are ubiquitous. No other medium is as influential."

Turning the idea into a reality proved to be difficult. The league board hesitated to make such a bold move and at first agreed only to a strictly religious film. It eventually agreed to a more subtle religious film, one that could draw a large audience.

In the mid-1980s, Courts at last began seeking a suitable script. He asked a California producer who once made league TV commercials to solicit scripts from literary agents. More than 150 poured in — many full of violence and sexual encounters. Few were remotely close to being suitable.

Unsure what to do next, Courts asked a sailing friend about possible writers. "Why not Lee David Zlotoff?"

"Who?"

Zlotoff wrote *Hill Street Blues*, a gritty, acclaimed TV show, and created *MacGyver*, another heralded TV series about an unconventional hero who does not use a gun.

Zlotoff came up with a story idea within three weeks. The script had no car crashes, gory murders, or wanton sex. It presented three-dimensional characters, a compelling plot, and a heart-rending story line. Far from being preachy, the script subtly explored issues of forgiveness and redemption.

Courts formed Gregory Productions, named after Fr. Gregory Bezy, the league founder. The league lent the production company several million dollars. The film's budget eventually hit $6.1 million — high for an independent film but low for a major motion picture. Shooting in Vermont took just a little over a month. Ellen Burstyn, Marcia Gay Harden, and Alison Elliot, the film's leads who were well-known actresses, agreed to accept relatively low salaries.

The Spitfire Grill is set in Gilead, a small, sleepy town in Maine where a young woman, recently released from prison, is hired as a waitress at the town's diner. She is able to change her life and the lives of others in Gilead.

Making a wonderful film is one thing. Getting it noticed and released in many theaters is another. The film's big break occurred in 1996, not long after it was made, when the prestigious Sundance Film Festival in Utah agreed to show it, one of eighteen chosen from among five hundred entries.

Festival audiences wept. The movie won the Audience Award as the festival's best film. Industry executives lined up with checkbooks in hand. The most ever paid for an independent film shown at Sundance had been $2.5 million. Castle Rock Entertainment agreed to fork over $10 million to distribute *The Spitfire Grill*.

Most reviewers liked the film, and it grossed $28 million. One reviewer described it as "a valentine to the human heart."

The league decided to use the profits to replace creaky Sacred Heart School in Southaven, the only Catholic school in the county. Built after World War II, seven classrooms were in trailers, intended to last ten years but in use for thirty. The cafeteria tripled as a gym and an auditorium. A small brick building served as the library.

The new $6.1 million school building was dedicated in 1999. The sixty-thousand-square-foot building housed sixteen glistening classrooms, a computer lab, a science lab, a fine-arts room, a large gym, and a chapel. The central courtyard included benches for outdoor classes, and a sixteen-acre nature preserve surrounded the school.

Enrollment immediately jumped by 100 to 370. Many students received financial aid that now was available. The building was financed by the producer's $3.5 million profit, with the rest donated by the Sacred Heart priests.

Today the school enrolls 333 students. Many still receive tuition assistance. Nearly a third of students are children of color.

The students who initially benefited from the movie never watched it at school. Its content was considered too adult for them. But the movie loomed over the school. Above the school's cafeteria entrance, emblazoned in red neon, are the words "The Spitfire Grill."

LATE-NIGHT TV

Late-night TV is Catholic country. Jimmy Kimmel, Jimmy Fallon, and Stephen Colbert are Catholic. All were altar boys and partook of the sacraments. Although their job is to be funny, they take their faith seriously.

Their comedy is not mean or cruel. Though they have their own comedic styles, they favor silliness over insults and find humor in life instead of indulging in sarcasm and contempt. To varying degrees, they do not hesitate to make light of the shortcomings of the famous and powerful. But they typically poke fun at someone or something without a nasty edge. They carry a certain generosity of spirit. It's not hard to credit their spiritual *joie de vivre* to growing up amid a belief in the Incarnation.

The silliest of the trio, Fallon, has made faces with Jude Law, played Pictionary with Kristen Bell, and danced to hip-hop with Justin Timberlake. As a boy in New York, he considered becoming a priest. One of his most cherished childhood memories is attending early-morning Mass with his grandfather. When Pope Francis visited the United States in 2015, his show tried to get the pontiff for a chat and almost succeeded, he said.

Colbert is the most upfront of the three about his faith, which he reclaimed in his twenties. As a young man, not sure about his future, he had decided God was not real. But that all changed in a moment, as he shared with *America* magazine.

Shivering while walking on a cold night in Chicago, he was handed a pocket Bible by a stranger. It had an index listing verses to be read depending on one's emotional state. Beset by anxiety, Colbert turned to a Bible verse for that difficulty. It turned out to be from the Sermon on the Mount: "Do not worry about your life, what you will eat or drink; or about your body, what you will wear. Is not life more than food, and the body more than clothes? ... Can any one of you by worrying add a single hour to your life?"

Colbert was instantly transformed. "My life has never been the same," he said. He often carries the Bible with him and says he equates God with love.

A practicing Catholic, Kimmel is not shy about standing up for what he believes. A few years ago, he got into a Twitter spat with Roy Moore, who was running for the U.S. Senate and accused of sexual misconduct. Moore accused Kimmel of mocking his Christian values. Kimmel took umbrage: "I happen to be a Christian, too. I made my first Holy Communion. I was confirmed. I pray. I support my church. One of my closest friends is a priest. I baptize my children."

STEVE CARELL

Michael Scott of *The Office* is a well-dressed schlemiel, someone who thinks he fits in but invariably fumbles the ball in interacting with others. His Prison Mike shtick embarrasses a new employee who is an ex-con, and he tries to make Oscar, the gay HR staffer, feel welcome by awkwardly and cringingly smooching him in front of the entire office. The upside is that, despite Michael's manifest faults, his employees like him. He may not have a heart of pure gold, but they know he has a heart.

It stands to reason that it takes a decent person to portray him, and

Steve Carell is, by all accounts, a gem of a person. Actors, writers, and others who worked on the TV show are unabashed in their admiration and praise. "I knew Steve in my days at Second City in Chicago. He was hilarious, very shy and very kind. … The show did not change him one bit," says Kate Flannery ("Meredith") in *The Office: The Untold Story of the Greatest Sitcom of the 2000s*. Amy Ryan ("Holly") concurs: "He's such an approachable, warm person." Adds a costume designer, "Steve is truly the loveliest man in Hollywood."

Born in Concord, Massachusetts, Carell was the fourth son in a Catholic family. His father was an electrical engineer and his moth-

er a psychiatric nurse. They were both devoted to their children, he says. Carell played the fife, competed in hockey, and studied history in college. He nearly became a lawyer. But after his father casually asked what he actually enjoyed, he decided to become an actor.

Carell prefers not to talk about his faith at length, other than to say he is Catholic. He and his wife dote on their two children. A journalist who profiled him wrote that he talked about his children incessant-

ly. "I think at the end of my life I'm not going to think: 'Oh, I did that TV show or that movie.' It will really have to do with how I raised my kids," he said.

About a decade ago, in Marshfield, Massachusetts, where he and wife spend part of the year, he bought a small general store. It had been in business for more than 150 years, but its future was shaky. He bought it to maintain it as a community hub. The previous owner seconded what his Hollywood friends know: "He's a lovely guy, very down to earth."

EVERYBODY LOVES RAYMOND

The popular sitcom *Everybody Loves Raymond* was based on Ray Romano's dysfunctional Catholic family in Queens. His TV mom, Marie Barone, played by Doris Roberts, was meddling and pushy. His TV dad, Frank Barone, played by Peter Boyle, was loudmouthed and irascible. Romano has joked that his TV dad was not far removed from his real dad: "Anything you see Peter Boyle do on TV, my father has done in real life without pants on."

In real life, Romano attended Catholic grade school and high school. Not only did his sitcom at times place the faith of the Barones front and center, but the cast was probably more deeply rooted in Catholicism than any other network comedy ever.

In one episode, angry at his parents, Ray sits down with the priest at his church. He feels he has broken one of the Ten Commandments by not honoring his mother and father. When the priest realizes that it's Frank and Marie Barone that Ray is describing, he forgives him instantly.

Born in 1935 in Philadelphia, Peter Boyle graduated from La Salle College. He joined the Christian Brothers Order and entered a house of study as Brother Francis. He later recalled praying "so hard I had calluses on my knees." He left the order and became an actor, memorably playing the bumbling, can't-dance monster in *Young Frankenstein*.

As father and son on the sitcom, Boyle and Romano enjoyed some classic generational Catholic conflict. In an episode titled "The Prodigal Son," the two argue over Ray's failure to go to church.

FRANK BARONE. He never goes to Mass, Marie. It's an open-and-shut case. ...
MARIE. You should go to Mass, Raymond.
RAYMOND. I don't want to go.
MARIE. Why do you hurt me?
RAYMOND. Look, I don't mean to hurt you, Ma.

FRANK. Stop hurting your mother. Go to church. ... Look what you're doing to her. Go to church.

RAYMOND. No. No. I don't feel like it.

FRANK. "I don't feel like it." That's the problem with you kids today. Everything has to feel good. You think World War II felt good? ... Twelve years of Catholic school down the toilet. Go to church.

Patricia Heaton, who played Ray's wife, Debra, grew up, in her own words, "a devout Catholic." Her parents were daily Massgoers. She took with her into her public life a commitment to her values. In 1998, she was honorary co-chairwoman of Feminists for Life. Five years later, she walked out of the 2003 American Music Awards telecast, before her scheduled appearance, in disgust over the language and behavior of some presenters.

Her public stances earned her enmity. A California radio personality posted caustic remarks about her: "I'm Patricia Heaton, and I'm a religious zealot who thinks she knows what's best for everybody." A *New York Times* story about her, though sympathetic, was headlined "Not Everybody Loves Patricia."

In between takes on the set, Heaton and Boyle, who were at opposite ends of the political spectrum, traded jibes. Romano said he usually hurried away "to see what the new doughnut was at the craft table." But their disagreements were good-natured. After Boyle died, Heaton sat in a pew at his service and sobbed uncontrollably.

JOKE WITH THE POPE

Jews often are considered the kingpins of comedy. But Catholic comedians are legion: the two Bobs, Hope and Newhart; Bill Murray; John Belushi; Chris Farley; John Candy; and Tim Conway, the rubber-faced, rubber-legged regular on *The Carol Burnett Show*, to name a few. Conway prized his faith, but he had fun with it too. He joked, "I like to go into the confessional and stay for an hour and a half. And just let people wonder."

This book is about people and things you might not know were Catholic, but there is one person you certainly assume is Catholic but is not. The "honorary comedic adviser to the pope" is a Jew. Even better, he's a rabbi.

Rabbi Rob Alper won the Joke with the Pope contest in 2015. The Pontifical Mission Societies in the United States launched the contest in advance of the pope's visit to the United States. The society, which spreads the Catholic faith overseas, encouraged people to "donate" a joke to support one of three needs overseas.

Bill Murray was named the honorary adviser for pontifical comedy to the society, and Conan O'Brien, a Catholic, donated a joke early to help the contest gain visibility. His joke: "The California drought is so bad, people in Napa are asking the pope to change the wine into water."

Pope Francis supported the contest by issuing a statement through the society: "I like to laugh. It helps me to feel closer to God and closer to other people. When we laugh with each other — and not at each other — God's love is present in a special way."

He added, "I invite you to share your joy with a laugh! God longs for you to be happy! Share your jokes and your funny stories: the world will be better, the pope will be happy, and God will be the happiest of all."

The contest netted four thousand submissions. Rabbi Alper topped them all with this: "My wife and I have been married for over forty-six years. Our lives are totally in sync. For example, the same time I got a hearing aid, she stopped mumbling."

BOB NEWHART

Few people who knew Bob Newhart in 1958 would have ventured to guess he'd be a comedian. Or that an album of comedic monologues he released on April Fool's Day in 1960 would reach number one on the Billboard pop chart, the first album to do so, and win a Grammy.

Even stranger, the album was, like Newhart, understated and almost quiet. This was the era of Lenny Bruce and his acerbic, expletive-laden style. In striking contrast, *The Button-Down Mind of Bob Newhart* included a deadpan bit titled "Abe Lincoln vs. Madison Avenue."

Just two years previously, Newhart had been an unknown advertising copywriter. Before that, in an even more exciting job, he worked as an accountant for United States Gypsum.

Like Hemingway, Newhart was born in the Chicago suburb of Oak Park in 1929. His father was a plumber and heating worker. His mom stayed at home with Bob and his three sisters, one of whom became a nun. Bob attended Catholic grade school and, in Chicago, Saint Ignatius College Prep and then Loyola University, where he studied business management. He was button-down Bob.

His road to comedy began when he and a co-worker, because of the tedium of their jobs, carried on humorous phone conversations for laughs. They recorded them and sent them to local radio stations, but no one was interested.

After his coworker left for another job, Newhart deftly adapted the routines for one person. A deejay liked his new versions and shared them with the head of talent at Warner Bros. Records. Before long, Newhart was a star.

A decade or so later, he was a TV fixture, starring as a Chicago psychologist named Bob in *The Bob Newhart Show* during the 1970s and as a Vermont innkeeper in the 1980s series *Newhart*.

Newhart does not spare his faith in his comedic jabs. "In the Catholic religion, as you know, we have confession," he told graduates at the 1997 commencement of the Catholic University of America in Washington. "And non-Catholics don't really understand how we go into this dark little room and say the terrible things we've done. But if you are raised Catholic, there are certain tricks you learn: you sit in the very last pew and you watch the two lines move, and whichever moves the fastest, that's the one you get into. We've all done that."

Being from Chicago, he also jokes about the fanaticism over Notre

Dame football. The best time to go to confession is during a game. "You can tell the priest anything: I just killed my family. 'Well, don't do it again, my son.' You could hear the game on in the background."

Newhart and his wife have been married for sixty years and raised four children. "Being Catholic has a lot to do with it. You work a little harder. You don't just have your first fight and walk out the door," Newhart told *Legatus* magazine. "I don't care how successful you've been in this business, if you haven't had a good family life, what have you really achieved? Not an awful lot."

KELLY RIPA

For years, the upbeat TV talk-show host Kelly Ripa spent her mornings chatting up celebrities. The glamour ended when she crossed her threshold. She and her husband, actor and onetime soap opera costar Mark Consuelos, raised three children close in age. Like so many parents before them, they decided their Catholic faith would help ground their brood. The family went to Mass together, prayed together at night, and said grace before meals. "You realize you want your kids to grow up the same way you did. [Religion is] a stabilizer in a young life. It gives you a foundation," Ripa told a magazine. Going to church was not a chore but a blessing. "We've been so fortunate that the least we can do is go and say thank you and be reflective for an hour," she added.

IX

SPORTS

In the movie *Chariots of Fire*, based on a true story, Eric Liddell is a divinity student in the 1920s who can run long distances faster than any other man alive. He recognizes where his gift comes from. For him, the tie between sports and God goes much deeper than gratitude for athletic prowess. He confides in a friend, "When I run, I can feel His pleasure."

Sport connects us to God. "Heaven is a playground," wrote G. K. Chesterton. That notion goes all the way back to the Book of Genesis. When Adam and Eve were driven out of the Garden, they were forced to toil. Work replaced their play.

Play is the province of the spirit. When we play, we indulge in pure spirit and in the joy of creative spontaneity. "I was beside him, like a master workman; / and I was daily his delight," proclaims the Book of Proverbs, "rejoicing before him always, / rejoicing in his inhabited world / and delighting in the sons of men" (8:30–31).

The basic meaning of *spirituality* helps explain how sports and spirituality are inseparable. The Latin root of the word is *spiritus*, meaning "aliveness." Being spiritual means being super-alive, or very much aware of life. The spiritual life is not about making us religious, according to Fr. Thomas P. Ryan in *Wellness, Spirituality and Sports*, but about helping us realize that we are already deeply religious. Through a spiritual attitude, a heightened sense of awareness of the sacredness of every activity, especially one as enlivening as sports, becomes a form of prayer.

Catholics who went to Catholic school can probably recall the young priest on the playground or the ball field. Sure, he was just being friendly, but his presence also revealed an instinctive understanding of the highly charged spirituality wrapped up in the shouting, the scampering legs, and the frenzied play.

The Church has held sports in high regard down through the ages. Our religious heritage emphasizes the dual nature of humanity. We're body and soul. We believe in the Incarnation, that the Word became flesh. We are made in the image and likeness of God. God is part of every human activity, especially one that is so tied up in our physicality.

TWO ANCIENT SAGES
OF PHYSICAL FITNESS

Saint Irenaeus, a bishop who laid the foundations of Catholic theology, preached on the dual nature of humanity around the year 200. He wrote: "For that flesh which has been molded is not a perfect man in itself, but the body of a man, and a part of a man. Neither is the soul itself considered apart by itself, the man, but it is the soul of a man. Neither is the spirit a man, for it is called spirit, and not man. But the commingling and union of all these constitutes the perfect man." As with other early Fathers of the Church, Irenaeus adhered to the philosophical tradition of Socrates, Plato, and Aristotle, who promoted physical fitness to bring body and soul into harmony.

The great theologian St. Thomas Aquinas also wrote of the importance of the body in attaining spiritual gifts. He held that we learn through the senses. The body needs to be disciplined so the mind can be disciplined in its search for truth. St. Thomas Aquinas's words echo what the ancient Greeks taught about exercise laying the foundation for spiritual vitality.

NUMBER-ONE SAINT-ATHLETE
OF ALL TIME

The earliest and most notable saint-athlete of all time has to be Saint Paul. We don't know for sure what sports he played, but there is plenty of evidence that he was an athlete. Paul was fond of sports metaphors. His most famous sports analogy is: "I have fought the good fight, I have finished the race, I have kept the faith" (2 Tm 4:7). In this and other passages, Paul comes off as someone who was closely familiar with athletics.

Other parts of Paul's identity suggest an athletic background. He was a Hellenized Jew, and the Greeks, the originators of the Olympic Games, cherished athletic competition. Also, Paul's conversion on the road to Damascus supposedly occurred while he was on a horse, so he was an equestrian. His tireless journeys around the Mediterra-

nean promoting the new faith stamp him as an athlete too.

If Paul was a jock, he was a thinking man's jock. He knew that there was so much more to life than sports. He wrote, "Do you not know that in a race all the runners compete, but only one receives the prize? So run that you may obtain it. Every athlete exercises self-control in all things. They do it to receive a perishable wreath, but we an imperishable" (1 Cor 9:24–25). Down through the ages, parents, coaches, and teachers have cautioned their ball-loving charges that sports must be kept in perspective. Consider Paul the bedrock source of that admonition.

BOWLING

Bowling began as a religious ceremony held in the cloisters of churches in Germany. In the third and fourth centuries, German peasants carried a wooden club, similar to the Irish shillelagh, for protection. As a catechetical version of turning a sword into a ploughshare, monks placed the club, called a Kegel, a fair distance from a parishioner. Since, in those days, the world was imbued with religion and ordinary objects were part of the divine drama, the Kegel represented a heathen. The parishioner rolled a stone at it in an attempt to knock it down. Success meant freedom from sin.

The game developed variously. Some keglers played with three pins, and others with as many as seventeen. The game's popularity persisted even with clergy. Martin Luther built a bowling lane

for his children and, while not busy with his ninety-five theses, threw an occasional ball.

After the Civil War, a number of Catholic churches in the Northeast and the Midwest had bowling areas built within them. Bowling alleys were associated with gambling and drinking, and the German immigrants wanted a safe place for family recreation. Some of these church alleys still exist.

LACROSSE

Baseball is considered America's pastime. But a game relished by Native Americans can be more properly considered our country's first sport, and its name has a decidedly Catholic origin. In the 1630s, a French Canadian missionary watched the Hurons use a stick to swat an object. The stick reminded him of a bishop's crosier, a staff shaped like a shepherd's crook. In his journal, the priest called the game *le jeu de la crosse.*

Lacrosse, America's oldest game, has a second association with Catholicism, which honors everyday actions as opportunities for grace and holiness. Lacrosse was so important to Native Americans that they used it to settle disputes between tribes, and the Iroquois even buried a player alongside his stick. It was more than a game to Native Americans. It was considered a gift of the Creator, whom they played to please.

PAPAL JOCK

In modern times, the most famous Catholic athlete was surely Pope John Paul II. As a young boy in Poland, after his father pushed the furniture to the side of the room and produced a rag ball, Karol Wojtyla engaged in spirited one-on-one soccer games. He was such a nimble goalie at school that his classmates called him "Martyna," after a famous soccer star. With his friends, he took long hikes into the Beskid Mountains, and on rainy days, he and his best friend played ping-pong.

As pontiff, he hiked, skied, and swam. Shortly after becoming pope, he had a twenty-five-meter swimming pool built at Castel Gandolfo, his summer residence. When someone questioned him about the cost, he impishly replied that "a pope needs to exercise." Besides, he added, the pool was less expensive than holding another conclave.

Pope John Paul II frequently praised the value of sports. During the jubilee year 2000, the Vatican orchestrated a Jubilee of Sports. The pope proclaimed, "It is a fitting occasion to give thanks to God for the gift of sport, in which the human person exercises his body, intellect and will, recognizing these abilities as so many gifts of his Creator."

Youth was always a paramount concern of the pope, and he addressed the significance of sports to young people. "Playing sports has become very important today since it can encourage young people to develop important values such as loyalty, perseverance, friendship, sharing, and solidarity."

The pope also found in athletics an exact parallel to the struggle for holiness. Great athletes sacrifice for years on end to achieve their goals. "This is the logic of sport. It is also the logic of life: without sacrifices, important results are not obtained or even genuine satisfaction." But even the most outstanding athletes will ultimately fail without God. "The greatest champion finds himself defenseless before the fundamental questions of life and needs [Christ's] light to overcome the demanding challenges that a human being is called to face."

Pope John Paul II's association with sports was so strong that Topps, the maker of baseball cards, issued a special, one-of-a-kind card of the pope in April 2005, just in time for the baseball season. The card featured his autograph and a short biography but, alas, no photo of the pope schussing down a slope or making waves in the Vatican pool. The card, which had no photo at all, was discovered by a California man in an ordinary pack of baseball cards. A collector bought the card for a price in the four figures.

The pope swam until he was well into his eighties. He granted audiences to athletes such as Muhammad Ali, soccer star Ronaldo, and the Harlem Globetrotters. When he died in 2005, in an acknowledgment of his love for sports, the Italian soccer league canceled all its matches, and the top finishers in a Grand Prix race refrained from spraying champagne on the victory podium.

The pope's passion for sports outlived him. Shortly before the Olympic Games in Greece in 2004, he had begun at the Vatican a new office dedicated to Church and sport. In a statement heralding the sports department, the Vatican acknowledged the importance of sports in contemporary life and said its new office would serve as both a tool of evangelization and a means to promote the positive aspects of sports.

Number-One Sports Fan in Rome

As a boy in Argentina, Jorge Mario Bergoglio was a goalie in football (soccer) games and also, like his dad, played basketball. But he was not a natural athlete, "born with two left feet," as he lamented. Sports was not his calling. He became a priest, of course, and now we know him as Pope Francis.

As a busy priest, he often could not follow sports as closely as other fans. In 1986, Argentina, led by Diego Maradona, was in the World Cup. The future pontiff was in Germany, working on his doctoral thesis and learning German. He found out the next day that his team had won "when a Japanese boy wrote on the blackboard [during our German lesson] '*Viva la Argentina*,'" he told a journalist.

As with any other fan, it was hard to be so removed from the action. Sports taught the pope — the hard way — the value of community and friends. "It was a difficult time for me," he said. "Personally, I remember it as a victory of loneliness, because I had no one with whom to share the joy. Isolation makes you feel lonely, while what makes happiness beautiful is being able to share it with someone."

An avid sports fan, Pope Francis continues to root for the favorite team of his boyhood, the San Lorenzo soccer team in Argentina. One of his treasured childhood memories is when San Lorenzo won a championship game when he was ten. "I remember those days spent watching the players and the happiness of us boys, when we returned home: the joy, the happiness on our faces, the adrenaline in the blood," he said.

Known for his modest lifestyle as he rose in the Church — such as taking a bus and not having a driver — Pope Francis did indulge himself a bit when it came to sports. Years ago, he donated one hundred dollars to build a new stadium for San Lorenzo. In thanks, he received a piece of a seat from the old stadium. He left that piece of wood in his office in Buenos Aires when he left for Rome in 2013 to vote in the conclave that elected him.

SEVENTH-INNING STRETCH

One of the most endearing traditions of the game of baseball is Catholic-related. A native of Kilkenny, Ireland, Christian Brother Jasper Brennan was in charge of student discipline at Manhattan College in New York. He set up a baseball program at the school to channel the students' energy, and he attended the games to keep a close eye on the young men. At a game in June 1882 against a semipro team, he saw trouble brewing. The young fans started to get out of hand during the long game. So, as his team came to bat in the seventh inning, he had the students stand up and stretch for a few minutes.

The strategy worked. The students settled down after the time on their feet. The seventh-inning stretch soon became a tradition at the college. It caught on in the major leagues when Manhattan played an exhibition game in the old Polo Grounds against the New York Giants. Their fans stood when the Manhattan fans did. The tradition gained a firm foothold in professional baseball in 1889 during the seventh inning of the World's Championship Series between the Giants and the Brooklyn Bridegrooms.

"Casey at the Bat"

The Mighty Casey struck out — but strictly as a ball player, not as a Catholic man. And, in reality, Casey never even went to bat.

"Casey at the Bat" has been one of the best-known poems in American literature since it was published in 1888 in the *San Francisco Examiner*. Ernest Thayer, who wrote for the *Examiner*, penned it and based it on a high school classmate back in Massachusetts.

A practical joker as a teenager, Thayer was a classmate of Dan Casey — tall, powerful, and not reluctant to put up his fists when angered. He was just the type of lad Thayer could not resist chiding. In the school's newspaper, Thayer crafted a story about a student he called Mr. Casey, who struggled with Latin. Casey's classmates teased him about it, and the bearish student angrily confronted a classmate in a hallway, picked him up, and turned him upside down.

Everyone at Worcester Classical High School knew that Thayer had based his fictional character on their lumbering Irish classmate with a big temper that matched his physique. So when the real Casey walked down the halls, students could not resist reciting a few lines of Thayer's piece. Casey had enough and confronted Thayer with balled fists but refrained from striking him. He then marched menacingly toward the underweight school editor, who shivered with fright. Again, Casey held his temper in check and stomped off without throwing a punch.

Casey knew how to keep calm when distressed. He put a hand in his pocket and fingered a rosary. A devout Catholic, his mother had urged Dan to carry a rosary and to ask the Blessed Mother to help him make good decisions.

Thayer's poem became a staple of vaudeville, and a 1906 recorded version popularized it further. One generation after the next embraced it. Walt Disney released a recording after World War II, and decades later came other popular versions: the Cincinnati Symphony Orchestra with Reds star Johnny Bench, quirky baseball pitcher Tug McGraw with Peter Nero, and the Philly Pops and James Earl Jones.

Baseball was central to America, as was its exaltation of the individual, and the poem was poignant and sweet about a man's very public failure. But its wistfulness transcended borders. British actor Sir Derek Jacobi with the National Symphony of London recorded one of the best versions of the poem.

As for Casey, he had learned to control his temper and do the right thing. He became a beloved teacher and principal in Worcester schools. "All the children loved him," said a colleague.

Casey didn't live to see much of the hoopla. He died in his early forties in 1915. A fellow principal in Worcester remarked, "If he had gone to bat in that game, he never would have struck out. He was a winner."

The fact is, Casey didn't even play baseball. Thayer had wanted someone memorable as his protagonist, and he remembered the tall, muscular student who made him tremble in high school. In 1930, Thayer reminisced about the time Casey confronted him after he needled him in Latin class: "He didn't like it, and he told me so. His big, red hands turned white at the knuckles."

But the mighty Casey, fingering his rosary, never struck.

BABE RUTH

The annals of American sports history are filled with heroes and superstars who were Catholic. The biggest Catholic sports icon of all time has to be Babe Ruth, who towered over his sport more than Michael Jordan or Tiger Woods did over theirs. Ruth remains a sports legend a century after his golden era as a home-run king. But he was seemingly destined for a life of crime and poverty, if not for the Xaverian religious order and a religious brother among them whom Ruth hailed as "the greatest man I've ever known."

Born in 1895 in Baltimore, George Herman Ruth was an unruly child who began skipping school as soon as he started and ran with a tough crowd of young boys through the alleys and streets. His mother was tired and often sick, and his father was preoccupied with running a tavern. Unable to control their son, the Ruths turned him over to St. Mary's Industrial School for Boys. On his application he was described as "incorrigible."

The Xaverian Brothers at St. Mary's housed, fed, and schooled eight hundred boys, many of whose parents had died, divorced, or abandoned them. Ruth became a practicing Catholic at St. Mary's and served regularly as an altar boy.

As an adult, Ruth never would have been described as an "altar boy." He was fond of women, liquor, and food and often treated people cruelly. But he also had a sunny side. He was generous with his time and

money, and he especially liked children — visiting hospitals, orphanages, and children's wards in cities where the Yankees had ball games. St. Mary's had provided a highly disciplined environment that steered many boys away from trouble and toward responsibility and generosity, and the "incorrigible" young Ruth was one of them.

The prefect of discipline was Brother Matthias, the person Ruth admired more than any other. Brother Matthias was a huge man, standing six feet six inches tall and weighing more than 250 pounds. Years later, when Ruth took his Yankee teammates to visit St. Mary's, they posed for a photo with Matthias. The Yankees were strapping athletes, but Matthias made them seem small and shriveled. His stature helped him get the attention and obedience of the boys at the home without hitting them or even shouting. The young Ruth was loud, boisterous, and aggressive. Matthias took a liking to him and took him under his wing.

The brother also helped mold him as a baseball player. The Xaverians believed in the benefits of sports not only to maintain the boys' health but also to impart social and moral values. There were more than forty baseball teams at the home. Matthias hit fungoes to Ruth and the other boys. Ruth claimed he could hit from the moment he first picked up a bat, but he credited Matthias with teaching him how to field.

Ruth began his major league career as a pitcher and soon became one of the dominant pitchers in the majors before concentrating on hitting. Matthias had turned him into a pitcher too. One day, Ruth, a catcher, was mercilessly taunting his pitcher after giving up one hit after another. Matthias had seen enough. "All right, George, you pitch. Show us how it's done," he said.

Ruth signed a pro contract with the Baltimore minor league team when he was twenty. The owner had seen a St. Mary's game against another team. The school was his legal guardian, so the Brothers had to agree to "parole" Ruth. His St. Mary's teammates stood outside the school office as the details were finalized. "There goes our ball club," one of them lamented. Matthias shook his hand and quietly said, "You'll make it, George."

Ruth went on to smash every home-run record. Included were his "called shot" in the World Series against the Cubs and homers he hit for desperately ill children. He also once hit a homer to benefit a Catholic church. In September 1923, while the Yankees were driving for a pennant and Ruth was fighting for a batting title, an assistant pastor boldly asked the star for a favor. Ascension of Our Lord Parish in Philadelphia had just built a new ball field and was struggling to pay for it. Knowing that children used the field, Ruth agreed to take part in a charity game.

Getting to the church on time would require a small miracle, however. The Yankees played the Philadelphia Athletics at 3:15 p.m. The charity game had to begin by 6:00 since the field had no lights. Incredibly, Yankees pitcher "Sad Sam" Jones threw a no-hitter. The Babe hopped into a cab and made the game on time.

More than ten thousand fans squeezed into the stadium, and hundreds more packed the nearby hills. Ruth did not disappoint. Playing against a team sponsored by a department store, he ripped a monstrous six-hundred-foot shot well over the fence. The umpire, however, not one to be intimidated by a legend, ruled it a double because of the short right-field fence. Ascension lost the game 2–1, but Ruth's box-office magic retired the debt and gave the parish memories for a lifetime.

Catholic Golden Age

In baseball's golden era, during the late 1940s and 1950s, Catholics predominated. More than half of the four hundred or so major leaguers were Catholic, including some of the biggest stars: Joe DiMaggio, Stan Musial, Yogi Berra, Gil Hodges, and Herb Score. A Catholic almanac

in that era even named a Catholic All-Star team each year.

What gives? Was it because Catholic immigrants played the game with a passion as a way to climb out of poverty, much as Latino players did decades later or Black players did with basketball? Or was it because the game flourished in old Catholic cities such as Boston, Chicago, Cincinnati, Cleveland, and Philadelphia? Or was it because, as columnist Robert Novak once speculated, baseball encouraged and taught teamwork, a core principle embraced by immigrant Catholics as a way to fully realize an American identity?

No one can say. Polls in the postwar era showed that Catholics loved baseball more than any other religious group. The Catholic ballplayers, in turn, treasured the game and the opportunities it afforded them, some decidedly spiritual. As just one example among many, Joe Garagiola, an ordinary major leaguer who went on to a Hall of Fame broadcast career, got to meet with Bishop Fulton Sheen in Brooklyn after Mass. The celebrated priest, a radio and TV star, gave him and Musial crucifixes.

Years later, Garagiola's house was robbed, and his World Series ring and crucifix were taken. Those were "my two greatest losses," he said.

Nevertheless, "One of the greatest blessings baseball gave me was the chance to meet Bishop Sheen," said Garagiola, who grew up in a humble St. Louis home praying the Rosary in Italian with his parents. "He was a major influence in my life."

JOHNNY UNITAS

Johnny Unitas set passing records, won championships, and drew raves from Baltimore Colts teammates and fans for his unflappable leadership. He also was known for his old-school look: black high-tops and flattop haircut. The reality matched the appearance; he was a "square." Late in his career, as a San Diego Charger, he curiously opened a closed

locker-room door to see what his teammates were up to and quickly fled the room, wanting nothing to do with their "funny cigarettes."

He grew up in Pittsburgh in the 1930s with his mom, Helen, who was a fervent Catholic. After Sunday Mass, she and the children often stayed to walk the Stations of the Cross. Young Unitas fell in love with the Notre Dame football team. He checked out a library book on coach Knute Rockne so many times that the librarian ran out of room to stamp a return date. She finally just gave him the book.

A star at St. Justin High School, he visited South Bend and tried out for the team. The coaches liked his arm but told him that, at 137 pounds, he would not be able to take the pounding. Luckily, the University of Louisville offered him a scholarship. A coach promised his mom he'd graduate and attend Sunday Mass. Unitas fulfilled both parts of that pledge.

Baltimore was a Catholic city, and an astonishing twenty-two of the thirty-three players on their beloved, close-knit football team happened to be Catholic. Coach Weeb Ewbank was not Catholic, but he spent Sunday mornings on his knees with his Catholic players at Mass.

The players' identification with their faith was strong — so strong that a strange religious-related incident was a footnote to the famous 1969 Super Bowl. A few days before the game, Joe Namath, the brash quarterback of the New York Jets, ran into Colt kicker Lou Michaels at a bar. The two got into a heated argument over which one was the better Catholic. They nearly came to blows — which could have altered the course of football history if Namath had gotten hurt and not been able to lead the famous upset over the Colts.

Unitas remained committed to his faith, even as his legend grew. In his last season in Baltimore, the Colts and the Oakland Raiders happened to attend the same Mass hours before the game. Soon to be locked in combat on the field, thirty Catholics sat on each side of the aisle. Unitas strode forward to receive Communion. A Colts coach whispered to the team's assistant general manager, "Look at the way the Raiders are staring at him. They're in awe of him."

Unitas died in 2002. His funeral was held in Baltimore at the Cathedral of Mary Our Queen. His gritty ace receiver, Raymond Berry, spoke on behalf of the team. A Protestant, he was perplexed about what to say, especially because Unitas had been a private man who rarely got personal. "I started praying about it. 'God, you've got to give me some clarity on this. You're the only one who really knows Johnny U.,'" Berry recalled.

Berry stuck to what he was certain was true: "All of us are glad God gave you the body to be a quarterback. I guess it is appropriate to thank the Lord, not only for your talent but for sending you to Baltimore to bless all of us. … I came to love you like a brother. Because of your life-long faith in Christ, you now have experienced the truth of Scripture — to be absent with the body is to be present with the Lord."

VINCE LOMBARDI

When Tom Brady, Patrick Mahomes, or anyone else raises the Lombardi Trophy after winning the Super Bowl, they are recalling one of the greatest coaches of all time — and one who was absolutely committed to his faith. Vince Lombardi, the legendary coach of the Green Bay Packers, put God first. He attended daily Mass, went to confession several times a week, and dropped to his knees every morning to pray before statues of Saint Anthony and Saint Jude.

Lombardi grew up in Brooklyn with a deeply religious mother. Daily prayer was a routine in their home. Lombardi's parents held priests in high esteem. His mother had him deliver to the rectory the bread she baked, and young Vince sat beside his father when his father swapped stories with the parish priests on visits to their home.

After eighth grade, Lombardi attended a high school seminary. He was certain he would become a priest, but that was not to be. He became a football star at Fordham and decided he wanted to get married, have children, and stay in sports. For eight years, he was a football coach and teacher at St. Cecilia High School in Englewood, New Jersey. He taught physics, chemistry, and Latin while coaching a team in 1943 that outscored opponents 267–16 and was widely regarded as the best high school team in the country.

In choosing a career in sports, he was not turning his back on pursuing holiness. The Jesuits at Fordham had taught him the value of discipline, hard work, and striving for a greater good. According to David Maraniss in *When Pride Still Mattered*, Lombardi had absorbed the ethos of Ignatius of Loyola, the founder of the Jesuits. Football was just a game. But it was a way to achieve a higher ideal. Lombardi would strive for excellence in sports. His ego would serve a greater good. He believed that the skills required in football — duty, obedience, responsibility, and attention to detail — would help him become a better person and keep him on the path to heaven.

Lombardi's faith was never far from him as he climbed the coaching ladder. As assistant with the New York Giants, he received an offer to be head coach of the Philadelphia Eagles. He prayed over it for hours in a church. To be a head coach was his ultimate professional goal. But it didn't feel right in his heart, and he declined the offer.

Other opportunities came along, and Green Bay proved to be a perfect choice for a devout Catholic such as Lombardi. The city was heavily Catholic. The Packers' preseason training camp was held at St. Norbert College in De Pere. Lombardi quickly befriended the "White Fathers," as the Norbertine priests were known because of their white robes. On game days, Lombardi gave sideline passes to several priests. Much of his fifty-ticket allotment went to nuns he and his family knew.

Lombardi kept his faith ever before him, even as he drove to practice. He draped snap-on rosary beads over his steering wheel so he could recite the Rosary on his way to work.

His players came from a variety of religious backgrounds, and Lombardi did not think it was right for him as a coach, with the power to cut players or demote them to the bench, to proselytize. He only infrequently referred to God or religion in his fiery pregame pep talks. But his players knew what drove him. They often joked among themselves about what mattered to their coach more: winning the game or getting to heaven.

His faith was evident in his support of Black players. In an era of racial intolerance, Lombardi's commitment to equality galvanized the team. He welcomed Black players at a time when many of his peers didn't. His disdain for discrimination was personal. He had been bullied for his Italian heritage and for being Catholic while growing up. The Packers credited their coach with creating a "brotherhood" on the team, no easy task in the racially charged 1960s.

Lombardi's storied teams won two Super Bowls. But, to him, football was about holiness, not winning. "We have God-given talents and are expected to use them to our fullest whenever we play," he told a diocesan newspaper. The newspaper extolled Lombardi for understanding his job as a calling. His approach to sports displayed the "profound, but often ignored admonition that everything we do should glorify God, and we glorify God the most when we 'put out' the most in whatever occupation or profession we have chosen."

Lombardi's faith imbued his routines and habits, even the famous "Lombardi time" precept. The Packers knew that rule: If you didn't show up fifteen minutes early for a meeting, you were considered late. The rule is so associated with Lombardi and the Packers that the giant timepiece affixed to Lambeau Field in Green Bay is deliberately set a quarter hour ahead of the correct time. That urgency never to be late goes way back to Lombardi's days as a conscientious altar boy: young Vince made sure always to show up an hour early when he served Mass.

THE "HAIL MARY"

A "Hail Mary" is a long pass in football, thrown out of desperation late in a game. The phrase became popular thanks to its utterance by the iconic Catholic quarterback of the Dallas Cowboys.

In 1975, Roger Staubach was the leader of the NFL's most visible team. Throughout his career, he had been celebrated not only for his football skills but also for his modesty, his moral rectitude, and his devotion to his faith, family, and nation. In 1963, as a quarterback for Navy, he won the Heisman Trophy as the best college football player. He dutifully served for four years in the navy, including a tour in Vietnam.

When he returned to the States, he quickly made up for lost time on the field. He eventually led the Cowboys to four Super Bowls, winning in 1972 and 1978. But his most memorable moment came in a 1975 playoff game against the Minnesota Vikings. With time winding down, he lofted a desperate fifty-yard heave toward the end zone. Drew Pearson caught the pass for the miraculous last-second win.

Swarmed by reporters in the locker room, Staubach was asked about the wild pass. "Well, I guess you could call it a Hail Mary. You throw it up and pray," he told them.

Staubach's stature, as well as the importance of the playoff game, popularized the phrase, and it's now commonly attributed to the Cowboys' quarterback. But, in fact, the expression goes back at least to the 1930s and Notre Dame's legendary Four Horsemen. According to Jim Crowley, one of the four, in a 1922 game against Georgia Tech, Fighting Irish players had prayed the Hail Mary before two plays. Both resulted in touchdowns. After the game, lineman Noble Kizer, a Protestant, told Crowley, "Say, that Hail Mary is the best play we've got."

VIRGINIA MCCASKEY

The Chicago Bears practice at Halas Hall, near the city, and inside the complex is a well-appointed chapel. A gleaming crucifix is mounted behind the altar. There are stained-glass windows and chairs with kneelers. The Bears chapel is believed to be the only one in an NFL facility.

Knowledgeable Bears fans are not surprised that the Monsters of the Midway make room for a quiet devotional place. Virginia McCaskey, the ninety-nine-year-old owner of the Bears, is a daily Mass-goer. She prays the Rosary each evening. She gives crèches to disadvantaged families in December and, throughout the year, hands out thousands of rosaries, colored blue and orange — the colors of her beloved team.

There may be no more humble Catholic in sports than McCaskey. The Bears, one of the most iconic sports franchises, are worth an estimated $3.5 billion, but McCaskey lives in the same modest suburban home she has resided in for decades.

She is the daughter of NFL legend George Halas, the original owner of the Bears and the cofounder of the NFL. She took over the team after he died in 1983.

McCaskey had a front-row seat to the NFL's rise to the top of the sports world. She accompanied her dad on the Red Grange Barnstorming Tour in 1925 and watched the team as it brought innovation to football with the T-formation and hoisted the Super Bowl trophy in 1985 after Walter Payton, Jim McMahon, and William "Refrigerator" Perry ran roughshod over the rest of the league.

Her father attended Mass, even on game days, and went to Confession on Saturdays. McCaskey similarly puts her faith first. "Football, the Super Bowl, these are all great things, but there are many more important things in life," she said.

Prayer is at the center of her life. "I couldn't get through a day or a night without praying the Rosary," she said.

SIMONE BILES

Olympic gold medalist Simone Biles never left her home in Texas for competitions without a rosary and a statue of Saint Sebastian, the patron saint of athletes. She was also rarely without her trademark determination, discipline, and, of course, extraordinary skills. Those traits vaulted her into the rare air of being one of the top gymnasts of all time. She hauled in thirty-two Olympic and World Championship medals, making her the most decorated American gymnast and tied as the world's most decorated gymnast.

She achieved all this despite a difficult childhood. Her parents in Columbus, Ohio, struggled with addictions. When she was six, her grandparents, Ronald and Nellie Biles, adopted her and her younger sibling. Homeschooled in Spring, Texas, Simone once trained thirty-two hours a week. Sunday was her day off, so she could attend church with her grandparents. Her mother gave her the rosary she carries.

Simone treasures her faith. As she recounted in her autobiography, when she received the sacrament of confirmation, "I marched into St. James the Apostle Church that Sunday in a line of teenagers with solemn faces. Our procession reminded me of a medal ceremony, except that no gold, silver, and bronze medals would be given out. Instead, our prize would be something much more powerful: in a few moments, each of us would bow our heads to receive the Holy Sacrament of Confirmation."

KATIE LEDECKY

Katie Ledecky became a household name, at least among fans of the Olympics, when, as an unknown fifteen-year-old, she unexpectedly won a gold medal in the eight-hundred-meter freestyle in the 2012 London Games. Four years later, in Rio de Janeiro, the swimmer took home four gold medals and a silver as she set two world records.

She is known for her bright smile, her humility, and her staunch Catholic faith. She prays before racing. "The Hail Mary is a beautiful prayer, and I find that it calms me," she told a Catholic newspaper.

Growing up in Bethesda, Maryland, she attended Catholic grade school and high school. Her family cherishes their faith. Her godfather is a Jesuit priest.

Ledecky was a longshot to make the Olympics team in 2012. Unlike many others in the extremely competitive world of youth swimming, she was not someone who single-mindedly focused on swimming from an early age. Until she was eleven, she took Irish dancing lessons.

She has won seven Olympic gold medals and ten overall, and her dominance was reminiscent of the transcendent Michael Phelps, the most decorated Olympian of all time. Yet she does not have Phelps's freakishly long torso or other obvious physical advantages. Ledecky once took a battery of physical tests at the American Olympic Training Center to determine what possibly could explain her success. "The findings are remarkably unremarkable," the report concluded.

A crowd of students, teachers, and staff from her high school greeted her at the airport when she returned from the 2016 Games. "Her swimming really doesn't define her as a person, which is what I think keeps her grounded," said a school official. "She is so lovable."

Kobe Bryant

Kobe Bryant could be tyrannical and aloof, and the sexual assault charge against him should temper any assessment of his life. But he also was a devoted friend and mentor to many, and his love for his daughters was boundless. A lifelong Catholic, Bryant said frank discussions with a priest after the criminal charges helped him get through that time. Bryant attended Mass on Sundays and sometimes during the week. On January 26, 2020, he took his daughter Gigi to 7:00 a.m. Mass, and later that day fatefully boarded a helicopter with her.

X

Outer Space to Cyberspace

We live in a secular society. A wall divides church and state. Government enterprises, especially ones that involve billions of taxpayers' dollars, can't endorse religion or give play to spiritual practices. But Americans savored the moment on Christmas Eve 1968 when the crew of Apollo 8 read from the Book of Genesis as their spaceship circled the tranquil blue earth.

The very first "meal" on the moon was not freeze-dried steak or even a glass of Tang. On the Apollo 11 mission in 1969, Buzz Aldrin, an Episcopalian, took out a Communion wafer, poured wine into a chalice from his church, and celebrated the Lord's Supper.

Something about space invites spiritual reflection. We look up toward the sky and see heaven. The grandeur of the stars suggests the majesty and perfection of God. When John Glenn, the first American to orbit the earth, returned to space in 1998 at age seventy-seven on the shuttle *Discovery*, he remarked, "To look out at this kind of creation and not believe in God is impossible."

While we once deemed space as the final frontier, now cyberspace is the region of limitless possibility. Whereas space can seem cold and remote to the earthbound, cyberspace takes us deeper into the here and now. It opens new vistas for connection and community. The phone, the airplane, and the television reduced our world to a global village. The internet squeezes us even more tightly together. Despite the manifest serious problems posed by social media and false information, the internet offers the promise of a village in which people know their neighbors on the far side of the globe better and interact with one another as equals before God.

MOON CRATERS

The flights to the moon may seem to represent the apotheosis of rational, scientific thought, completely divorced from the work of the Church. In fact, Jesuits in particular have distinguished themselves as scientists and mathematicians through the centuries. No fewer than thirty-five craters on the moon are named after Jesuit scholars. These are not minor or insignificant craters, either. Some of them are large enough to be seen by the naked eye.

OBSERVATORIES

The Vatican was one of the most influential supporters of astronomy for centuries. In the early 1500s, Pope Gregory XIII, intent on reforming the calendar, built a tower to facilitate solar observations and employed mathematicians to confirm predictions about the equinoxes. The papacy also established three of the earliest observatories in or near Rome, the first in 1774.

The modern-day Vatican Observatory was built on a hill behind St. Peter's. The growing city lights soon made that location impractical, and in the 1930s, the observatory was moved to Castel Gandolfo, the pope's summer retreat enclave, about twenty miles from Rome. The scientist priests who work there are considered world class. The obser-

vatory's meteorite collection, including bits of Mars, is among the world's finest as well.

The Vatican opened a second observatory in 1993 in the desert, on a remote mountaintop two hours from Tucson, Arizona. The Vatican Observatory Research Group operates at the Mount Graham International Observatory. Over the years, many of the astronomers, astrophysicists, and mathematicians at the observatory have been Jesuits. The Vatican's highly sophisticated telescope there is one of the world's most powerful. The plaque erected near it when it was dedicated reads in Latin: "This new tower for studying the stars has been erected on this peaceful site. May whoever searches here night and day the far reaches of space use it joyfully with the help of God."

The late Fr. George Coyne, the Jesuit who directed the Vatican Observatory from 1978 to 2006, explained why the Church bothers with astronomy: "It's a glorious participation in God's creation to try and understand it. The more we understand it — if you have religious faith — the more you understand God, since he's the source of it."

ASTRONAUT THOMAS JONES

Catholic means "universal," and the Faith has not been confined to earth's gravitational pull. A number of astronauts have been Catholic, and many have relied on their faith during their perilous journeys. If there are no atheists in foxholes, neither are they found in the cockpits of rockets. Thomas Jones of Oakton, Virginia, who spent fifty-three days in space on four shuttle missions, has spoken eloquently on his faith and floating in space.

Jones was a member of the *Endeavour* crew in 1994. A scientist with a doctorate in planetary sciences, he assisted the crew as they used radar echoes to map changes on Earth's landmasses and oceans. Before the flight, besides reviewing his financial records and his burial wishes, he met with his pastor for the Sacrament of Reconciliation. During

the final countdown on the launching pad, as his pulse raced and his breath shortened, he prayed for the safety of his crew and asked God to be with his family, who nervously waited and watched three miles away.

The takeoff was seamless. The "flaming torch," as Jones called his spaceship, climbed into space. A week into the mission, realizing it was Sunday, Jones and two other Catholic crew members gathered for a brief Communion service. The consecrated host had been carried aboard in a simple golden pyx. Moments after the three had shared the Body of Christ, dazzling white light burst through the cockpit windows. The sun had risen. The rays of light exposed the deep blue of the Pacific Ocean. Tears moistened Jones's eyes. One of the other astronauts, gazing at the dazzling color of the waters below, remarked, "It's the blue of the Virgin's veil, Tom."

Jones had come a long way from his days as a student at Our Lady of Mount Carmel School in Baltimore. But even while in space, he knew his place in the universe. He was "one unimportant astronaut." He felt a deep "humility at my miniscule place in God's limitless universe." The glory of God was as wide and deep as space. "Riding the prow of the Space Station, I thought of how much God had done for me. ... I thought, how limitless must be God's gifts to those truly in need."

ASTRONAUT RICK HUSBAND

Rick Husband (left in photo) was another devout Catholic astronaut. As a young boy, he played with toy airplanes and gazed spellbound at the heavens through a telescope. In a high school class in which he had to give a speech on his future career, he talked about orbiting the earth as an astronaut. Afterward in the hallway, his friends snickered, "Yeah, right. You're going to fly to the moon." But after being rejected three times for the space-shuttle program, he was finally chosen for a mission: the space shuttle *Columbia*. On February 1, 2003, the shuttle broke up as it returned to Earth, killing the seven astronauts on board.

Husband had been a scout, and the bishop of Arlington, Texas, celebrated his life during the annual diocesan scout Mass after the *Columbia* disaster.

Husband had seen something far more incandescent than stars when he peered through a telescope. He saw order and design. "There is no way you can look at the stars, at the Earth, at the moon and not realize that there is a God out there who has a plan and who laid out the universe," he insisted to a skeptical friend.

ASTRONAUT WILLIE MCCOOL

McCool also was aboard the fatal flight of the *Columbia*. A navy commander with vast experience as a pilot, McCool served as pilot of the *Columbia*. He was a convert to Catholicism. In 1993, a parish priest in Maryland baptized him. A solid, well-respected man, McCool was married with three boys. His conversion was not a matter of filling a hole in his life or turning over a new leaf after turmoil and trouble but was a step forward in his search for fulfillment. "I want to entrust my life to Jesus and see how high I can go, so he can love through me," he told the priest who baptized him.

While in space, McCool took time to email the priest. He described how the brilliant rainbow of colors down below on Earth contrasted with the blackness of space smeared with the light of a multitude of stars.

At his memorial service, Psalm 139 was solemnly read: "If I ascend to heaven, you are there. … Even there your hand shall lead me, and your right hand shall hold me" (8, 10).

TEACHER AND ASTRONAUT CHRISTA MCAULIFFE

As with the Kennedy assassination or September 11, many Americans can remember where they were when they learned that space shuttle *Challenger* exploded in 1986. The tragedy shocked Americans, who turned to one another for consolation. According to a study, more than 85 percent of Americans heard the news within an hour of the accident.

All seven crew members aboard died, including Christa McAuliffe, who would have been the first teacher in space. She had been selected by NASA from more than eleven thousand applicants to conduct experiments and teach lessons from space.

The oldest of five children, Sharon Christa Corrigan attended Marian High School in Framingham, near Boston, and taught confirmation classes at her parish, St. Peter's. Outgoing and daring, she played shortstop on her church's baseball team, played a nun in her school's production of *The Sound of Music*, and dreamed of going into outer space. After John Glenn orbited the earth in *Friendship 7* in 1962, she told a friend at Marian, "Do you realize that someday people will be going to the Moon? Maybe even taking a bus, and I want to do that."

McAuliffe was a social studies teacher at Concord High School in New Hampshire. Her selection as an astronaut did not surprise those who knew her as an outstanding teacher and exemplary person. "You knew she would win because, well, she was Christa," said the chairperson of her department.

She was thirty-seven when she died. Her cousin, a priest, who had celebrated her marriage sixteen years earlier, celebrated the funeral Mass at her hometown church.

THE SPACE WINDOW

Sacred space takes on a completely new meaning at the National Cathedral in Washington. (The cathedral is Episcopalian, not Catholic, but it does make a special effort to be ecumenical and welcome other faiths for certain events there.) One of the cathedral's magnificent stained-glass windows is dedicated to scientists and technicians. Known as the Space Window, it's rich with symbolism. Its small white dots represent stars. The thin white trajectory wrapped around a sphere symbolizes a manned spaceship.

But the star of the window is embedded in its upper center: a seven-gram basalt lunar rock from the Sea of Tranquility. The 3.5-billion-year-old rock is the size of a silver dollar. The *Apollo 11* crew — Neil Armstrong, Buzz Aldrin, and Michael Collins — brought back the rock from the moon. It's the only moon rock given to a nongovernmental agency. The base of the Space Window quotes Scripture: "Is not God in the height of heaven?" (Job 22:12). The lunar rock belongs to all.

CYBERSPACE VISIONARY

The *unofficial* patron saint of the internet is Marshall McLuhan, who, in the 1960s, coined the term "global village" and foresaw a world linked together through "electronic interdependence." The unassuming college professor was a prophet of the future, and his theories were deeply rooted in his Catholic faith.

Born in western Canada in 1911, McLuhan taught literature, communications, and other subjects at the University of Toronto and other colleges. His groundbreaking theories on modern communications were inspired by observing his children. They were engrossed by the new medium of television, while also giving their attention to the radio and reading. Their rich, multitasking approach to life suggested a new way to relate to others. Television especially was pivotal in this fresh interaction. Whereas, in the past, people gathered around the campfire to listen to stories, today's society increasingly revolves around the images beamed into a box in people's homes.

"The medium is the message," McLuhan famously concluded. How information is presented is as important as the content. The way stories are told changes us fundamentally.

His celebrity dimmed today, McLuhan — who died in 1980 — was once a cultural touchstone, quoted often in magazine articles and cited in books. His photo was featured on the masthead of *Wired*, precious to the digital generation. He made a cameo in Woody Allen's 1977 *Annie Hall*, espousing his thinking.

Not so well known was his Catholic faith and its connection to his theories. Brought up as a Baptist, McLuhan moved toward Catholicism while studying at Cambridge. In the confusing, chaotic pre–World War II era, Catholic intellectuals and writers such as Evelyn Waugh and G. K. Chesterton offered solace. The latter especially helped persuade him of "the wonder of the real world as created by God and full of meaning," according to writer and theologian John Janero. McLuhan also was impressed by the extent to which the Church fostered learning and culture through the centuries. After much prayer and discernment with a priest friend, he was finally baptized in 1937.

As a Catholic, part of a universal Church, it was not a huge leap for McLuhan to conceive of a global village. But the medium being the message is very Catholic, too, according to writer David King. McLuhan, though generally private about his faith, once wrote, "In Jesus Christ, there is no distance or separation between the medium and the message. It's the one case where we can say the medium and the message are in complete unison." In ancient times and today, whatever our tools and technology, sacramental grace is afoot.

Perhaps more so than anyone else in these pages, McLuhan is the avatar for this book and its multitude of examples of God's presence in the world. The clever Canadian came to his faith partly from an appreciation of the role of Catholicism in society's development, expounded theories on modern life that were grounded in his faith, and drew acclaim — but without a widespread understanding of the underpinnings of his theories.

Number-One Twiplomat

World leaders vie for attention in a crowded social media world. Pope Francis has nearly nineteen million followers through his @Pontifex Twitter account, more than the U.S. president. (*Pontifex* is Latin for "pope.") Twiplomacy, which ranks the impact of world leaders on the social media platform, once ranked the pope as the most influential because of his average of forty-one thousand retweets.

The pope also communicates digitally via Instagram, the social image channel. His account there, @Franciscus, has nearly nine million followers.

In 2019, Pope Francis unveiled his Click To Pray app. Catholics can click on the mobile phone app, or log into a website, and pray to support the pope's causes and their own. Appropriately, the app was launched a few days before Catholic World

Pope Francis ✓
3,926 Tweets

Follow

Pope Francis ✓
@Pontifex

Welcome to the official Twitter page of His Holiness Pope Francis

📍 Vatican City 🔗 vaticannews.va 📅 Joined February 2012

8 Following   **18.9M** Followers

Youth Day. The pope first displayed the app during his weekly address in St. Peter's Square. The priest standing next to him held an iPad, as the pope tapped the screen before the crowd below. Showing that even the pope treads cautiously around newfangled technology, he hesitantly asked the priest, "Did I do it?"

The Digital Vatican

The world's oldest institution embraces modern digital communications. Vatican News, the one-stop shop for information about the Holy See, offers video, radio, podcasts, images, news, and audio services in more than thirty languages. During Easter Week in 2020, as the coronavirus raged, Vatican News livestreamed major events on its YouTube channels with live commentary in six languages — plus, for the first time, a channel featuring a sign-language interpreter. All major papal Masses, liturgies, and services have been streamed online for years.

A few years ago, the Vatican redesigned its website "to more seamlessly reach followers through new social channels," according to Accenture, the high-powered U.S. consulting firm that undertook the initiative. "All this has created new familiarity with The Holy See, and has given Pope Francis a voice closer to the people. It has enabled the Vatican to not only create a new online identity, but a digital source of content … reaching believers of diverse cultures, all over the world."

The online version of the Vatican Apostolic Library was revamped too. The new site offered improved search functions and easier access to digital reproductions of documents.

The "modern" version of the Vatican library was begun in the fourteenth century, though the Church has preserved a library and archive since the fourth century. A papal bull in 1475 opened the library and archive to study by scholars. The library contains records from a "thousand cultures and a thousand languages," a library official said. Its current holdings include 1.6 million books, 180,000 manuscripts, 200,000 photos, 150,000 prints, and 300,000 coins and medals.

The Vatican has touted the advantages of "digital Catholicism." The Pontifical Council for Culture praised the internet for its "immense potential" to help the Church in her evangelical mission. Cyberspace "can be enormously helpful in spreading the Good News. This has already been proved by various promising initiatives the church has taken." On the negative side, the pontifical council also warned that the internet can be misused, as any tool or instrument of society can be. According to the council, the danger lies in a uniformity of messages, the lack of responsible feedback, and discouragement of interpersonal relations.

THE INTERNET SAINT

Saint Augustine, the fourth-century theologian, may have anticipated the internet nearly sixteen hundred years before it arrived on our digital devices. He proposed that God is a circle in which the center is nowhere and the circumference is everywhere. That reflection was mostly forgotten until recent years, when someone realized that Saint Augustine had managed to visualize the network of knowledge we know as the internet.

Yet Saint Augustine is not the patron saint of the internet. That honor belongs to Saint Isidore, a Spanish bishop who died in 636. Pope John Paul II made the declaration in 1997. While not tending to his day job of ministering to his flock and fending off the barbarian tribes threatening to overrun Spain, Isidore researched and wrote the twenty-volume *Etymologiae*. Not as extensive as the work by St. Albert the Great (chapter 2), it was the first rudimentary encyclopedia of human knowledge.

Saint Isidore's exhaustive work was the *Encyclopeadia Britannica* of its day and for centuries to come. The Dark Ages put a halt to unfettered learning for several generations, and Isidore's book remained the standard reference guide on a wide range of subjects throughout the Middle Ages. In fact, more copies of *Etymologiae* survived from those times than any other book, with the exception of the Bible.

The learned bishop detailed in his groundbreaking book the knowledge he painstakingly collected on animals, geography, languages, kingdoms, agriculture, legal systems, clothing, and furniture. Nor was he a quiet, docile scholar who limited to quill and paper his contribution to learning. He was an outspoken advocate for increased access to education, and he vigorously encouraged the Church to provide instruction in medicine, the law, and the liberal arts.

Today the internet and outer space both loom before us as vast regions, without fixed boundaries and tied up with our destiny in a most uncertain way. But centuries ago, brave champions of knowledge and learning such as Isidore moved forward, steadied by intellect and faith despite the events around them.

XI

IT'S A CATHOLIC
WORLD AFTER ALL

God's grace saturates the world. God is wrapped up in what we do. The books we write and read, the games we play, and the TV shows and movies we create and watch reflect our sacredness.

Call it what you will — a Catholic sensibility, a Catholic sensitivity, or a Catholic heart — Catholics evince their sacred identity. As we work, play, create, and love, we leave our Catholic mark. Yes, we know we are Christians by our love. We know we are Catholic by this ineffable but powerful orientation to our identity as children of God. We acorns don't fall far from the Catholic tree. Our roots may remain unseen, but they go deep and reach out for nourishment for the spiritual rain that falls from heaven.

Our culture has hallmarks and landmarks that, on the surface, are absent of a Catholic influence but in reality have been shaped and informed by Catholicism. We're the iceberg faith of America. We hover underneath the waters, which are far larger, more solid, and more substantial than believed. We may live in a secular age. But our times draw from decades and centuries ago, and the influence of the faithful who have gone before us reverberates and remains. The parts of the world colored by Catholics and Catholicism do not fade to black, as each day does, but instead, dawn anew with each generation.

HOBBITS

Oxford English professor J. R. R. Tolkien was correcting examination papers in 1937. One seemed duller than the next. Prompted by his unconscious mind and uncapping a creative wellspring that would change the world, he absentmindedly scribbled at the top of one exam "in a hole in the ground there lived a hobbit."

Encouraged by his dear friend, the Christian apologist C. S. Lewis, he began to write the book that became *The Hobbit* and led to the hugely successful *Lord of the Rings* seventeen years later, in 1954. Tolkien drew from his knowledge of the natural earth, his experience as a soldier amid the horrible slaughter of World War I, his fears of a second world war, and his deep-rooted Catholicism to create a strange, fascinating, heroic world called Middle Earth — full of not only wee hobbits but also elves, dwarves, and wizards.

Tolkien often cautioned against reading his books as allegory. He doth protest too much. That statement rings about as true as Twain's epigraph in *Huckleberry Finn*: "Persons attempting to find a moral in it will be banished." Tolkien once admitted that the Ring saga was a "fundamentally religious and Catholic work."

Born in 1892, Tolkien was only four when he lost his father, who died in South Africa of rheumatic fever. His mother, who had been an Anglican missionary in Africa, converted to Catholicism and raised her two sons as Catholic in Birmingham. She died of diabetes when Tolkien was just twelve. But she had wisely arranged for a priest friend to become his legal guardian.

Tolkien spent thirty-nine years as an English don. He fit the part. He was a gentle, professorial man who smoked a pipe, rode an old bicycle, and took long walks. There was something of the hobbit about him. One student claimed he walked "as if on furry feet."

His circle of educated friends formed an ad hoc literary society that they called the Inklings. They gathered around a fire with a pint or two and read epic Norse poetry, shared manuscripts, and bantered about literature and religion.

Tolkien was instrumental in Lewis's progression from agnosticism to Christianity. Tolkien, in turn, leaned on Lewis to sort out his ruminations on myths and religion. All cultures seemed to use myths to explain creation and history, Tolkien observed. Christianity was "the perfect myth" since it encapsulated the best part of other myths — while, of course, being historically true, as Tolkien believed.

Tolkien's interest in myth was not merely academic: he was scarred by World War I and needed to make sense of suffering. His unit suffered heavy casualties. Only one of his closest friends was left alive.

Tolkien's faith was integral to his identity and the way his life unfolded. He often went to confession. As with Lewis, he was openly apostolic. In private, he was steadfastly pious.

His faith affected his marriage, for good and bad. His wife, Edith, agreed to convert when they married. But she resented going to confession and attending Mass and disapproved of Tolkien's taking their children to Mass. The marriage grew strained until they agreed that Edith should return to Anglican services. That calmed the marital waters, and their marriage lasted fifty-five years. They were both ecstatic when one of their sons became a Catholic priest.

Tolkien believed the Arthurian legends beloved by the English were weak compared with Norse legends and Homeric epics. He hoped his fantasies would serve as the preeminent English myths. He was glad that Bilbo Baggins, Frodo, Gandalf, and the rest of his characters could at least provide an escape from frightening realities. We need fairy tales to let us think about something other than factories, machine guns, and bombs, he said in a lecture in 1938.

But Tolkien was also purposely pursuing something much deeper. He deliberately drew on Catholic theology in crafting Middle Earth. His characters are not all good or all bad but are engaged in a divine drama. The moral contours of Middle Earth mirror our own. Reviewing *The Fellowship of the Ring* in 1954, the poet W. H. Auden wrote, "If one is to take a tale of this kind seriously, one must feel that, however superficially unlike the world we live in its characters and events may be, it nevertheless holds up the mirror to the only nature we know, our own."

MOZART

The Mozart depicted in the film *Amadeus* is foul-mouthed and feckless. Then there's that laugh, that ridiculous laugh. Geniuses certainly have their quirks, we conclude.

Well, the real Mozart did use scatological humor in his correspondence. But the Amadeus of Hollywood was quite unlike the real Amadeus, who was not infantile or even juvenile. He could be a little over the top, but he was grounded in a diligence to his talent and a seriousness in his faith.

It should be no surprise Mozart was devoted to his faith. He composed highly celebrated Roman Catholic Masses and more than sixty pieces of sacred music. Then-Cardinal Joseph Ratzinger (later Benedict XVI) praised Mozart:

"His music is by no means just entertainment; it contains the whole tragedy of human existence."

Mozart's music is a staircase to God. "I find it very, very hard to believe that the fervor and expressiveness of the music Mozart wrote for the church, such as the 'C Minor Mass' or the 'Requiem,' is just the equivalent of an opera composer making a good pitch for his libretto," Robert Levin, a Mozart expert at Harvard, told journalist John Allen. "The sense of the glory of God is so powerful. Mozart's spirituality emphasizes majesty, grandeur and affirmation."

Mozart embraced his faith. He once told a friend that an "enlightened Protestant" could never understand what the Agnus Dei of the Catholic Mass meant to him.

Mozart's parents, Leopold Mozart and Anna Maria, were fervent Catholics. They encouraged family prayer, fasting, the veneration of saints, Mass attendance, and frequent confession. When Amadeus was twenty-one, his father wrote to him: "God must come first! From his hands we receive our temporal happiness, and at the same time we must think of our eternal salvation."

Mozart assured his father of his steadfast faith: "God is ever before my eyes. I realize his omnipotence and I fear his anger; but I also recognize his love, his compassion, and his tenderness toward his creatures. … Thus all will be well, and I must be happy and content."

HUMMELS

Hummels, the German-made figurines of happy, chubby-cheeked children, are popular collectors' items. Hummels are based on the whimsical sketches of a Franciscan sister whose art was banned by the Nazis in Germany. The happy-go-lucky sister drew the ire of Hitler himself, who railed against the children with the "hydrocephalic heads."

Berta Hummel was born in 1909 in a small, picturesque village in Bavaria, a heavily Catholic area. Just down the road from the home of her large family was Oberammergau, the site of the famous Passion Play. Young Berta was known for her cheerful temperament. *Hummel* means "bumblebee" in German, and friends said the name fit her perfectly. She buzzed around with a zest for life.

Berta also was a gifted caricaturist, even as a youngster. "Sketch me, Berta," her little friends begged. Her father wanted her to be an artist or at least an art teacher. At age eighteen, she enrolled at the prestigious Academy of Applied Arts in Munich, where she lived in a boarding house run by two Franciscan sisters. The community of 250 sisters valued the arts. Many were teachers. Berta's father worried that becoming a sister would ruin her as an artist, but she listened to her calling to become a religious.

Becoming Sr. Maria Innocentia Hummel did nothing to quell her sunny disposition or her high spirits. Other sisters gently corrected her: "Will you ever learn to walk sedately?" Or "Please step quietly!" She was a bit like Maria von Trapp, the former novice in *The Sound of Music*.

She taught art at the convent school. As a reward for good work, she gave her students original picture cards, surely one of the best teacher tokens of all time.

The sisters, impressed with Hummel's talent and in need of income, sent her work to a Munich publishing house that specialized in religious art. The company reproduced some of her paintings as postcards, a popular medium in Germany. In 1934, it also published a collection of her drawings, called simply *Das Hummel-Buch* (*The Hummel Book*).

Fortuitously, one of the book's first buyers happened to be a craftsman at a porcelain factory. The factory owner agreed with his worker's bright idea: recreate Sister Maria Innocentia's drawings as porcelain figures. Sympathetic to the plight of the factory workers, who worried the factory would close, Hummel agreed.

Interest in the figurines exploded after they were displayed in 1935 at the Leipzig Trade Fair, a major international trade show. Hummel visited the factory often to oversee the work. One day, a factory worker rose and effusively thanked her for saving their jobs. Despite her success as an artist, she remained humble. Once a woman on a train reading *The Hummel Book* noticed her habit. She asked her if she was from the same community as the artist. "Yes, I am," she modestly replied.

Hitler despised her art because he believed Germans were the master race, and her depictions of children in patched clothes engaged in frivolity incensed him. Despite the danger, Sister Maria Innocentia bravely produced art at the convent that could not be made public. She drew sketches that contained the Star of David and designed a cross with a menorah before it for the convent chapel.

The war years were difficult for Hummel and her community. The Nazis closed their schools and confiscated their motherhouse. Only a few dozen sisters were allowed to stay. Hummel lived with her family for a while before returning to the convent, where food was scarce and the building unbearably cold. "What we suffered was indescribable," Hummel's superior wrote.

Hummel contracted tuberculosis in 1944. French troops eventually liberated her region, but the sister could not regain her strength, At noon on November 6, 1946, at only thirty-seven, she died as the Angelus was ringing.

The popularity of Hummel figurines grew after the war as American soldiers stationed in Germany began sending the figurines home as gifts. Popularity increased even more when the figurines were sold by the Army PX system.

Hummel figurines are still based on the many charcoal sketches and pastel drawings left by the prolific Franciscan artist. Each new work is discussed with an artistic board at the same convent she entered in 1931. A percentage of the profits goes to the convent and supports the sisters' mission.

Sister Maria Innocentia lived and died in a time when "the force of evil seemed most determined to eradicate all that right-thinking men held sacred and inviolable," wrote U.S. Franciscan sister M. Gonsalva

Wiegand in a 1951 biography of her. The cheerful, talented nun was "an opposing force of purity and consecrated service. She possessed in herself the power to see the bright side of ordinary human affairs and translated it for the enjoyment and stimulation of her fellowmen."

VALENTINE'S DAY

Catholic schoolboys and schoolgirls, after indiscriminately passing valentines to classmates, are inevitably reminded by their teachers that Valentine's Day goes back to Saint Valentine. Yes, Catholicism is tied up with the day dedicated to love, but it's complicated. There are so many stories about this Valentine fellow, and so many explanations about how the holiday began, that uncovering the truth is an exercise in doubt and frustration. You just have to take a leap of faith and believe in one version or another. Love is a lot like that too.

Here is what is known. Officially recognized by the Church, Saint Valentine was a real person who died around A.D. 270. However, two centuries later, discounting the legends about him, Pope Gelasius I in 496 declared that he died as a martyr but his acts were "known only to God." By 1400, two new competing narratives had gained traction. Valentine was a priest who was beheaded near Rome by the emperor Claudius II for helping Christian couples wed. No, he was the bishop of Terni, martyred by Claudius on the outskirts of Rome.

The problem is that Valentine was a popular name. *Valentinus* is Latin for "worthy, strong, or powerful." Historians have found accounts of several Valentines who were martyred. A Pope Valentine even served in 827. The official roster of saints includes a dozen named Valentine or a close variation. The last one canonized was in 1988: St. Valentine Berrio-Ochoa, a Spanish Dominican who was beheaded in 1861 in Vietnam. The saint we celebrate on Valentine's Day is known officially as St. Valentine of Rome, to differentiate him from the other holy Valentines.

More uncertainty: It's possible Valentine's Day was a pagan ob-

servance "baptized" at some point by medieval authors. Romans celebrated the feast of Lupercalia from February 13 to 15 in honor of the god Lupercus, believed to protect pregnant women. Before the feast, young people pledged their love for each other or agreed to marry.

The custom of sending cards stems from a legend surrounding the original Saint Valentine, who died in 270. In this story, he was an Italian doctor who later became a priest and was imprisoned for performing weddings despite a ban on marriages. He fell in love with the daughter of his jailer and smuggled out a note to her.

The holiday also is linked to the great medieval English poet Geoffrey Chaucer. In his 1375 poem "Parliament of Foules," he ties the tradition of courtly love with the celebration of the feast day of Saint Valentine. The poem refers to February 14 as the day birds (and humans) come together to find a mate: "For this was sent on Seynt Valentyne's day / Whan every foul cometh ther to choose his mate." Until Chaucer wrote his well-known poem, the feast day was not associated with romantic love.

AA

Alcoholics Anonymous has rescued multitudes from misery. A priest saved the cofounder of AA from his terrible troubles and paved the way for the great success of AA.

The saga began with a knock on a door in New York at ten o'clock one night. "You have a visitor," the doorkeeper told Bill Wilson, the co-founder of Alcoholics Anonymous. Bill Wilson nearly sent the visitor away from the AA clubhouse in Manhattan without seeing him. He was in no mood to counsel someone presumably struggling with alcohol.

This was December 1940. AA had been founded five years earlier in Akron, Ohio, when Wilson met Dr. Bob Smith, who also was an alcoholic. The two had come to realize that working with other alcoholics was key to staying sober. Their group grew in fits and starts. In 1939, the group published *The Big Book*, which described their approach.

But Wilson was struggling badly again as Christmas neared in 1940. The book hadn't sold well. He and his wife had lost their home to fore-closure. Wilson had to move to the AA clubhouse. Even worse, a close friend of his in AA was drinking again and spreading ugly stories about Wilson among AA members. Wilson fell into a depression, a malady that dogged him.

The forty-two-year-old man who stood in front of Wilson that winter night walked with a limp and was roughly dressed. Wilson's assumption that his guest was an alcoholic appeared to be correct.

Then the man opened his peacoat, revealing a Roman collar.

Wilson's visitor was Jesuit Fr. Ed Dowling of St. Louis. Dowling's relationship with Wilson would prove to be decisive. It would help steady Wilson, help clarify and solidify the role of spirituality in the AA recovery program, and ultimately help AA grow and become the lifesaver for untold numbers of alcoholics.

Dowling walked with a limp because of rheumatoid arthritis. He was not an alcoholic, but he sometimes ate compulsively and to excess. He also smoked excessively.

Dowling's struggles made him empathetic to the difficulties of others. He had weathered his share of personal disappointments and setbacks. His journey to the priesthood had been anything but a straight line.

An exceptional baseball player as a youth, he tried out both for the Boston Red Sox and the St. Louis Browns, but neither team signed him. He studied journalism at Northwestern University and landed a job with the *St. Louis Globe-Democrat.* He then joined the U.S. Army in World War I. After the war, he entered the seminary but then abruptly quit. He struggled to understand what God wanted for him.

He taught at a Catholic high school near Chicago for three years before entering the seminary once again. This time it stuck. He took final vows in 1936. Assigned to the Sodality of Our Lady, he served as editor of its magazine, *The Queen's Work.*

Dowling had come to believe in the efficacy of AA. A friend had developed a drinking problem after losing his wife, and Dowling joined him at an AA meeting. But he didn't travel to New York just to testify to the value of AA. He quickly grasped that AA's twelve-step program had a lot in common with the Spiritual Exercises of Ignatius of Loyola.

Wilson had never heard of Ignatius or the Spiritual Exercises — so Dowling helped him understand that AA was on the right track.

The Jesuit renewed Wilson's spirit. "The curious little man went on and on, and as he did, Bill could feel his body relaxing, his spirits rising. Gradually he realized that this man sitting across from was radiating a kind of grace," explains the biography *Bill W.* "Primarily Father Ed wanted to talk about the paradox of AA, the 'regeneration,' he called it, the strength arising out of defeat and weakness, the loss of one's old life as a condition for achieving a new one. And Bill agreed with everything."

When Wilson admitted he was angry, impatient, and dissatisfied, Dowling had an answer. "Blessed are they who hunger and thirst," he replied.

"Can't I get satisfaction?" Wilson pleaded.

"Never. Never any," replied the priest.

Dowling reminded Wilson that he had "made a decision to turn his life and will over to God. He was not to sit in judgment on how he or the world was proceeding. It was not up to him to decide how fast or slowly AA developed. Whether the two of them liked it or not, the world was proceeding as it should, in God's good time."

Dowling was brilliant at spiritual counsel. Before he departed, he left Wilson with a final thought. Pulling his aching body up and leaning on his cane, the priest drew close to the AA cofounder and told him he had a force inside him, a force all its own. Don't mar it; don't block it, he urged. It won't exist anywhere again.

Wilson had been in turmoil before the unexpected visit of Dowling. That December was the dark night of his soul. Wilson's encounter with the hobbling priest was transformative for him. For the first time in many months, Wilson slept soundly. It was unlikely AA would have gained strength and numbers if he remained spiritually paralyzed and mired in depression.

Until that night, Wilson had been suspicious of Catholics. He and Smith had found some of their mojo from their connection with a Protestant spiritual movement called the Oxford Group. But from then on, Dowling essentially served as Wilson's spiritual director.

Dowling contributed to the next edition of *The Big Book* and thereafter championed AA among Catholics.

Dowling furthered AA, and AA and its twelve steps helped Dowling until he died in 1960. The priest used the twelve-step program to overcome his eating and smoking problems.

Besides boosting AA, Dowling made another major contribution to society. In 1942, he founded Couples Are Not Alone (CANA), which helped married couples in distress. The twelve-step methodology was a central component of the groundbreaking national movement. His knock on the door on that dark December night in 1940 opened doors for so many.

DON DRAPER

Devilishly handsome, Don Draper in the TV show *Mad Men* is a hot-shot Manhattan ad executive in the 1960s. His company is rife with carnality. His male colleagues drink, smoke, and bed women, often even at the office. As accomplished as he is at hawking consumer goods, Draper is even better at outperforming his coworkers in the carnal arts. He's a world-class Lothario in a crisp suit.

Mad Men conjures a curious world. Only one of the characters is identifiably Catholic: Peggy, a secretary who climbs the corporate ladder. A sole priest appears in a few episodes as a friend and quasi-mentor for her at her church. The creator of the show, Matthew Weiner, is not Catholic. Yet the show has a Catholic ethos: It's steeped in a Catholic imagination and grapples with sin, the wages of sin, and redemption.

Glamorous and glitzy on its surface, the series has a hidden skeleton: a Catholic worldview. It's as if a medieval morality play were grafted onto the streets, office buildings, and bedrooms of 1960s New York. Episode after episode, what the nuns told us in grade school plays out: You can accumulate wealth, drive fancy cars, live in upscale homes, and gain the hallmarks of success as set by society, but, without God, your life will ring hollow and empty.

A few times, the show veers off its secular course and lets slip the religion hiding beneath it. The ad men proposed a new pitch for Popsicles: "Take it, break it, share it, love it." Peggy remarks that the catchphrase sounds "very Catholic." She adds that the slogan is "Christian, in the social sense."

Draper, played by Jon Hamm (who grew up Catholic), epitomizes the shallowness of outward success. Hamm is brilliant in displaying two faces at once: the impossibly handsome corporate hotshot, whose wry, puerile grin at winning again in the corporate war room or in the bedroom is also somehow accompanied by a shadow of sadness, a glint in his eyes that seems to say, "Is that all there is?"

In one episode, Draper travels to California to meet with Anna

Draper, the only person who knows his real name is Dick Whitman. Anna is the widowed wife of the real Don Draper, who served with Dick during the Korean War. When Draper was killed in the war, Whitman, ashamed of growing up in a brothel, assumed his friend's identity.

The saintly Anna is the only person who knows Dick and loves him for who he is. Don/Dick confesses his identity struggles to her: "I have been watching my life. It's right there. I keep scratching at it, trying to get into it. I can't. … What does it mean?" She replies, "It means the only thing keeping you from being happy is the belief that you are alone."

Draper is literally and figuratively separated not only from God but also from his true self, from the person God meant him to be. Trappist writer Thomas Merton's insight is pertinent here: "Every one of us is shadowed by an illusory person: a false self. This is the man that I want myself to be but who cannot exist, because God does not know anything about him. … The secret of my identity is hidden in the love and mercy of God. … If I find Him, I will find myself, and if I find my true self I will find him."

Episode after episode, Draper seeks fulfillment in alcohol, sex, and work success, but happiness eludes him. He is disconnected from his true identity and flails helplessly at finding meaning and lasting satisfaction.

The opening credits suggest a spiritual underpinning to the show. Draper's silhouette is shown falling and tumbling. Robert Frost comes to mind: "That other fall we name the fall."

Draper's drama is not merely futile or pathetic. He comes close, again and again, to an insight or a breakthrough, only to fall short and fall down once more. Grace seems to be within his grasp, if only he knew how to reach for it and hold on. In one powerful episode, Bert Cooper, the kindly founder of the ad agency and a man apparently grounded in spiritual values, dies suddenly. The office mourns. As Don strides through his workplace, he hears, to his dumbfounded surprise, Bert's voice: "Don, my boy." He watches as Bert, along with several fetching secretaries, dances merrily and sings the song "The Best Things in Life Are Free." The vision fades, and tears fill Don's eyes.

It may seem easy to dismiss Draper as a reprobate. But his moral status brings to mind the remark of Dorothy Day when told she was a saint: "I won't be dismissed that easily." Draper a hopeless sinner? He can't be dismissed that easily. He's morally complex. He's lecherous but not unloving. He is sometimes an attentive, devoted husband and father. He's loyal, not treacherous, to his ad agency. He mentors and encourages, if sometimes awkwardly and harshly, his less-talented co-workers, including Peggy.

Though he typically succumbs to temptation, he wrestles with his conscience. You can almost see the battleground of his soul, the little red devil with the pitchfork on one shoulder and the white angel on the other.

As an ad man, Draper is selling the American dream that buying and owning things can bring happiness. He excels at what he does. His pitches are believable, even enticing. Early on in his career, in a campaign that established his bona fides, Draper has the task of promoting the new Kodak Carousel projector. He figures out a strategy. Before his presentation, he loads the projector with family vacation photos. This machine, he tells his awed client, is a "time machine," a way for families to remember and cherish their good times together.

His pitch is perfect. Family photos are wonderful vehicles for prying open warm feelings and uniting families. At the same time, Kodak gets its $129.99, and Draper is rewarded with a hefty paycheck and other prestigious clients. The problem for Draper and the rest of his ilk is that they celebrate their home run in the boardroom with more booze and women, failing to count or even consider their blessings.

In the final season, after numerous affairs, a ruined family life, and a teetering career, Draper's life spirals downward. He flees to a hippie-age retreat in California. He collapses in tears. He meditates on a hillside. In a brilliant piece of fictional chutzpah, the series ends with Draper, inspired by a dash of idealism, concocting the iconic Coke ad: "I'd like to teach the world to sing ..."

His ad is more than crass commercialism. It's a stab at higher ideals. Draper has enjoyed great worldly success. He hasn't turned his back on the world but faces it with a changed perspective. Mixed in with his desire to sell happiness in a Coke bottle is an earnest desire to do good. He has grown, moved forward, if only a smidgen. Great journeys begin with small steps. His is a pilgrim's progress. He may not drop to his knees at night or even think about God, but he has felt stirrings in his soul that at last got his attention.

AMERICA'S POET

"I think that I shall never see …"

Go ahead — complete the line. You surely can. Published in 1913, "Trees" became perhaps the best-known American poem of the twentieth century.

Joyce Kilmer, a Catholic poet killed in 1918 in France during World War I, wrote it. A college graduate who worked for *The New York Times* before serving overseas, Kilmer had no combat role. But he asked to be with his comrades on the front. He was on a scouting patrol when a sniper's bullet found him. He was thirty-one and left behind a wife and two children. He was awarded the French Croix de Guerre for bravery.

"Trees" was hardly Kilmer's only verse. At the time he enlisted, he was considered the premier American Catholic poet. Many of his poems, such as "Prayer of a Soldier in France," express his deep religious faith.

Kilmer considered himself an atheist until he was twenty-seven. He married Aline, a devout Episcopalian, in 1908, weeks after his graduation from Columbia University. Five years later, they both became Catholics. He once quipped that he had no choice because Catholics write the best poetry.

"Trees" first became popular in Catholic schools in the 1920s. Kilmer's status as a convert certainly helped give it traction. Its swaying rhythm also made it a popular choice at schools, where dramatic recitations were part of curriculums.

Another Kilmer poem with a bouncy beat, also popular among schoolchildren, was "The House with Nobody in It." It begins: "Whenever I walk to Suffern along the Erie track / I go by a poor old farmhouse with its shingles broken and black." Kilmer used to walk to Suffern to attend daily Mass.

"Trees" is routinely savaged by critics as lightweight verse, not on par with serious poetry. Maybe so; even the *New Catholic Encyclopedia* once weighed in that Kilmer's "poems and essays show promise rather than achievement."

Yet it may also be true that most of his poems have been forgotten because they deal with religion, and Kilmer might have matured as a poet if he had lived longer. In any case, Americans remember their war heroes. Innumerable schools, parks, and streets are named after Kilmer. The second-floor of his childhood home in New Brunswick, New Jersey, is preserved as a shrine to him.

Nor have Americans tired of "Trees." In 1999, when the U.S. poet laureate asked Americans to name their favorite poem, "Trees" made the top ten.

BARNEY

The ubiquitous purple dinosaur was all the rage for two decades, starting in the early 1990s, at least among two- to six-year-olds who watched PBS. The friendly, sunny Tyrannosaurus rex who danced and sang was dreamed up by a devout Catholic who was dismayed by the coarsening of children's entertainment.

Born in 1927, Richard Leach, a Chicago native, studied English literature at Loyola University and credited the Jesuits there with inspiring in him a moral vision. He got married, had nine kids, and ran Argus Communications, which produced audiotapes, books, and posters for a Catholic audience.

All things Catholic interested him. A visit to Assisi in 1987 led to an interest in Saint Francis, which led to a musical based on the saint's life.

Barney came about after Leach's daughter-in-law persuaded him of the need for a home video series that was educational and entertaining. Leach financed the first three videos with $700,000 out of his own pocket. The success of the videos led to *Barney & Friends*, which debuted in 1992.

The series eventually aired in more than a dozen nations, and the ever-cheerful purple dinosaur became part of the cultural landscape, a series praised by educators but often lampooned and ridiculed by those outside the two- to six-year-old demographic.

Undeterred, Leach in 1995 launched on PBS *Wishbone*, a show about a dog that reimagined great works of literature. Young viewers learned about such luminaries as Joan of Arc and Our Lady of Guadalupe.

Leach continued to develop programs of interest to Catholics, including an acclaimed five-hour documentary on the Second Vatican Council titled *The Faithful Revolution*. He also started a company called Developmental Learning Materials, which grew from his efforts to help his dyslexic son. Leach died of a heart attack in 2001 at age seventy-three.

THE MCCHARITY OF JOAN KROC, A MCCATHOLIC

There are multiple ways to start to tell the Cinderella saga of Joan Kroc. One is this: A salesman walked into a bar. Here's another: Can you blame the good Lord if a hard-driving, hard-drinking businessman departs this earthly home first, so a lady with a generous Catholic heart could inherit his McMillions and give a large part of the fortune away to good causes?

In 1957, Joan Smith, an attractive, vivacious blonde, was playing piano in a supper club in St. Paul, Minnesota, when she caught the eye of Ray Kroc, in town to pitch his new hamburger business. The volatile, charismatic entrepreneur was about to revolutionize the fast-food industry with his assembly-line techniques and low prices. Twelve years later, after he had divorced twice and she once, they married and moved from Chicago to San Diego.

Kroc died in 1984 and left his wife a baseball team — the San Diego Padres — and 6,700,000 shares in McDonalds. The daughter of a railroad worker, Joan was accustomed to scraping by until she married Kroc. Her husband had given away millions. But much of it was calculated to gain headlines and counter the notion that McDonalds was not healthy or good for society. Joan, on the other hand, chose people and causes that personally appealed to her.

The arms race and the possibility of nuclear war worried her. She spent $750,000 for newspaper ads with coupons addressed to the White House and the Kremlin. The coupon read: "Please stop all weapons testing immediately." When she secured a private audience with Pope John Paul II, she gave him a special cassette tape of a peace song commissioned for an upcoming Hiroshima commemoration. She whispered into his ear, "I am praying for the end to the arms race."

Not long after, in 1987, Fr. Ted Hesburgh came to San Diego to speak at a conference and talked about his dream of building a peace institute at Notre Dame, where he was president. Kroc was in the front row, and she hastily approached the priest after his talk. "How much would it cost?" Kroc asked Hesburgh, who had no clue who she was. "It will take six or seven million," he told her. "I'll send it to you in the overnight mail," she responded. That was the genesis of the Kroc Institute for International Peace Studies at Notre Dame.

Kroc liked and respected Hesburgh, so each year on his birthday, she dashed off a cheery greeting card and mailed it to Notre Dame. She never forgot to tuck in a check for $1 million. When he turned eighty-five, she sent him $5 million.

In her will, she left another $50 million for the peace institute at Notre Dame and $50 million for a peace center at the University of San Diego, a Catholic institution. She also gave several millions to the St. Vincent de Paul Homeless Shelter in San Diego.

During her lifetime and through her will, Kroc was generous with a variety of good causes: education, health care, AIDS and cancer research, youth programs, the arts, flood relief in the United States, and famine relief in Africa. She admired the cost-effective ways of the Salvation Army, so her will left it $1.5 billion. She was a big fan of National Public Radio, which received $225 million.

Kroc's giving was ecumenical, but Catholicism seemed always to hover about her efforts and concerns. Fr. Henri Nouwen, celebrated for his concern for those with disabilities, was her spiritual adviser. When he died suddenly on a trip to Holland, she sent a plane to return his body.

Joan's good friend was Helen Copley, the widow of a newspaper magnate. Copley was a devout Catholic, and she and Kroc traded notes on philanthropy. The two called themselves "the rat pack," a rat pack of generous Cinderellas.

Kroc died of brain cancer in 2003. Obituaries identified her as a Catholic. In fact, she had never formally become a Catholic, but her memorial service recognized her Catholic spirit. At her request, the bishop of San Diego led the service and Hesburgh spoke. The service was held in a garden behind the peace institute at the University of San Diego.

Placed amid the shrubbery was a sculpture of St. Francis of Assisi. Mourners received a prayer card. On one side was a picture of a younger Joan at the piano, and on the other was the prayer ascribed to Saint Francis: "Lord, make me an instrument of your peace ..."

SAINT BERNARD (THE DOG)

Around 1050, St. Bernard of Menthon set out to bring Christianity to the people living in the Alps, in what is now Switzerland. He founded a monastery and a hospice, located less than a mile from Italy. Yet getting to and from Italy was treacherous. The Great St. Bernard Pass is more than eight thousand feet above sea level and is typically covered with seven to eight feet of snow. Drifts pile as high as forty feet, and avalanches are common.

Around 1660, the monks at Great St. Bernard Hospice acquired their first dogs, the descendants of the mastiff-style dogs brought over by the Romans to serve as watchdogs and companions. The monks originally used the animals as guard dogs and as work dogs. One resourceful monk used them to power a rotating spit in the kitchen.

The Augustinian monks discovered that the dogs' broad chests allowed them to clear paths in the deep snow, and the dogs — now called Saint Bernards — soon accompanied travelers through the pass. The dogs' keen sense of smell also gave them the uncanny ability to discover people buried in snow. The dogs were trained to work in pairs. When they found a person, one licked him and lay down next to him to keep him warm, while the second Saint Bernard ran to the hospice for help.

The dogs were credited with rescuing two thousand people — from lost children to Napoleon's soldiers. Notwithstanding the popular representation, the dogs did their lifesaving work without barrels of brandy looped around their necks.

The last documented dog rescue was in 1897. Monks at the hospice now rely on helicopters. No longer needed, the eighteen dogs trotted out of the monastery for the last time in 2004. Yet authorities knew that

tourists identify the Saint Bernard with Switzerland, as they do chocolate or secret bank accounts, so the Saint Bernards now can be found at a kennel in a village down the mountain pass.

BINGO

It's no surprise that, when "Bingo!" is shouted, there's a good chance it's a person at a Catholic hall who is shouting. Indeed, a financially struggling Catholic church in Pennsylvania at the onset of the Great Depression helped popularize the game in the United States. It caught on so quickly at parishes that Catholics began joking in the 1940s that the next canonization would be that of Saint Bingo.

Bingo dates back to 1530 in Italy, to a lottery game that bore a vague resemblance to the modern version. In the eighteenth century, the French added playing cards, tokens, and the calling out of numbers. In the early 1920s, Hugh J. Ward created another version of the game that he called Beano. It became popular at carnivals in Pittsburgh and in western Pennsylvania.

Aside from some instances in Pennsylvania, Bingo in 1930 was played at home. The market was monopolized by the E. S. Lowe Company, thanks to the business savvy of Edwin Lowe, a New York toy salesman and the son of Jewish Polish immigrants. He produced two modest versions: a twelve-card set for one dollar and a two-dollar set with twenty-four cards. Lowe later developed and sold Yahtzee.

An unnamed priest from Wilkes-Barre, Pennsylvania, got in touch with Lowe. His parish was playing Bingo every week in the church basement to raise money. But there were so few cards that there were too many bingos and too many prizes to hand out.

Immediately sensing an opportunity, Lowe approached Columbia University mathematician Carl Leffler and asked him to create unique, nonrepeating-number Bingo cards. By 1930, Leffler was printing six thousand different Bingo cards. The priest's problem was solved. There were now exactly 552,446,474,061,128,648,601,600,0002,446,474,061, 128,648,601,600 possible Bingo-card combinations.

The church in Wilkes-Barre was able to keep open its doors. Bingo next saved a Knights of Columbus Hall in Utica, New York. By 1934, Americans were organizing ten thousand Bingo games a week, with Catholics leading the charge. Time after time, Bingo rescued churches in trouble. In 1939, St. Augustine Church in Cincinnati, despite being in a low-income neighborhood, raised an astonishing $220,000 from a weekly Bingo.

Bingo's success drew scrutiny from authorities, but it worked to the church's advantage. New York mayor Fiorello La Guardia feared that criminals would turn Bingo into a racket, so he banned it in 1938. New York legislators promptly passed a law that basically restricted Bingo to churches and synagogues.

Catholic bishops have disapproved of parishes' reliance on Bingo. In the 1980s, both Cardinal John O'Connor of New York and Cardinal Joseph Bernardin of Chicago came out against the game. The *Chicago Sun-Times* headlined the story about the cardinal's displeasure with the memorable headline: "Bernardin Bops Bingo."

But Bingo has outlasted them. Catholics enjoy playing a game to support their parish. That has been documented by academics — in 1986, in a report titled "St. Bingo," the Notre Dame Study of Catholic Parish Life found that only Mass attracts Catholics to their church more than Bingo.

A CHARLIE BROWN CHRISTMAS

"Isn't there anyone who knows what Christmas is all about?" pleads Charlie Brown on our TV screens each December. "Sure, Charlie Brown, I can tell you what Christmas is all about," Linus responds.

Linus proceeds to recite the Bible verses about the birth of Jesus. CBS executives feared that viewers would be turned off by the unabashed religious quality of *A Charlie Brown Christmas* when it first aired in 1965. They were historically wrong. Half of U.S. households tuned in. The TV special became a beloved American story, part of the cultural landscape, high on the list of the cultural canon of media. One critic called it "the greatest half hour American TV has ever produced."

In creating the show and anticipating blowback from CBS executives, Charles Schulz was insistent that the program convey the true meaning of Christmas. Otherwise, "Why bother doing it?" he asked.

Schulz was a churchgoing Protestant. Religion was important to him. One of his first jobs, as he struggled to pay the bills, was lettering the comics of a Catholic magazine called *Timeless Topix*. Later he taught Sunday school and even preached an occasional sermon from the pulpit of his Protestant church.

Schulz had a lot of help with the *Peanuts* Christmas special. Along with producer Lee Mendelson, a Jew, and jazz composer Vince Guaraldi, key to the magic of the show was an unassuming Catholic Mexican American, Bill Melendez. As head animator, he literally brought Charlie Brown, Linus, Lucy, Snoopy, and the rest of the characters to life and to a lasting immortality.

Melendez was born in 1916 in Hermosillo, Mexico. His father, a strict military man, wanted to name him Cuauhtémoc, after an Aztec emperor. The parish priest balked: "That's a heathen name." So he was christened José Cuauhtémoc and became known as Bill when he worked as an animator. Other animators preferred that name because it did not stand out so much and would not overshadow them in the credits.

His mother took him to the United States as a child, most likely surreptitiously crossing the border. Bill studied at what became known as the California Institute of the Arts. Walt Disney hired him in 1938 to work on shorts and such feature-length classics as *Pinocchio, Fantasia,* and *Dumbo.*

It was a good job, but Melendez was a man of principle. In 1941, he was a very vocal participant on a strike at the company over unionization. Disney backed down and recognized the union.

In the late 1940s, Melendez began working on commercials, doing hundreds, including one for Ford that featured the *Peanuts* characters. He met Schulz, and the two, both artists with consciences, became fast friends. Schulz came to value and trust his friend's rich but not overdone artistic style.

In 1963, Mendelson made an award-winning documentary about Willie Mays for NBC and had unsuccessfully pitched a documentary about Schulz to TV executives. By 1965, *Peanuts* was all the rage. *Time* did a cover story. A New York advertising executive asked Mendelson to ask Schulz about making a Christmas special.

Time was short; the Christmas special would have to be put together in a few months. Schulz wrote the outline in a single day. He and Mendelson quickly invited Melendez to join the team. The artist hopped on a plane to meet with the two. Creating the special under the tight deadline and getting it past CBS executives would prove to be something of a miracle in itself.

The team used children to voice the characters. The plan was to use a professional to "voice" Snoopy as well. But time was so short that Melendez recorded himself laughing, crying, and howling and then sped it up ten times. They had found the voice of Snoopy, a role Melendez reprised for all the *Peanuts* specials to come.

Good with kids, Melendez worked with the children who read the script in the studio. Some of them, including the child who played Linus, were too young to read. So Melendez patiently fed them their lines.

The show was put together in such haste that, as hard to believe as it is, Schulz's name was misspelled in the closing credits as "Schultz." Aside from that, Melendez and Mendelson were certain that they had failed and that the show was a flop. Their fears were not allayed by the stunned silence of CBS executives when it was screened for them. When they finally spoke up, the network bigwigs griped about the voices, the music, and the pacing. They just didn't get it. But its airing was scheduled for the next week — too late to make changes.

Buoyed by the stunning success of the Christmas special, Melendez went on to enjoy a long career in TV animation, including work on Garfield cartoons. He wasn't done with animation with a spiritual message. He won two Emmys for his work on a version of C. S. Lewis's *The Lion, the Witch and the Wardrobe.* He died in 2008 at age ninety-one.

The magic of the *Peanuts* special and its tenderhearted embrace of the meaning of Christmas live on. The birth of Jesus made manifest God's love. Linus knew that, just as he knew even a ragged little tree could thrive: "It's not bad at all, really. Maybe it just needs a little love."

IT'S A WONDERFUL LIFE

George Bailey had friends, the kind who pray. *It's a Wonderful Life* opens with prayers echoing amid the starry heavens. "I owe everything to George Bailey. Help him, dear Father." "Joseph, Jesus, and Mary, help my friend, Mr. Bailey." "George is a good guy, God. Give him a break."

As everyone knows, the movie's plot revolves around an angel,

Clarence, trying to "get his wings" by helping George, who misplaced the money of the "broken-down Building and Loan." Drowning his sorrow in a bar, George, played wonderfully by Jimmy Stewart, prays desperately to God. That moment of pleading gets him a bust in the jaw.

More religion comes when Bedford Falls residents "wept and prayed" on V-E Day and "wept and prayed" on V-J Day. People in Bedford Falls did a lot of praying in Catholic-like churches with grand exteriors and sweeping interiors.

Yet fans think of the movie not as one steeped in religion, or even a morality tale, but the story of a small-town decent man who loved his family and community and faced off against "a warped, frustrated old man." Clarence and all the other religious references seem like mere plot contrivances that advance the drama of an honorable man driven to a suicide attempt before recognizing the value of his life.

The movie is perhaps the most overtly religious popular film of all time. *It's a Wonderful Life* is not only a Christian film but essentially unfolds a Catholic vision of life.

The movie is director Frank Capra's deepest and most artistically satisfying expression of his rich Catholic faith, which was hard-won. Born in 1897, Capra was a self-described "Christmas Catholic" as a younger man. His brother was a priest, but Capra felt he needed God, well, only when he perceived he needed him. Early in his career, after failing to establish himself, he knelt alone in a back pew of a cathedral. He was there "to remind the Almighty here was another sacred sparrow needing help."

His career breakthrough came when he directed the highly successful *It Happened One Night* in 1934. Strangely, certainly to him, his triumph left him anxious as a director and hollowed out as a man. Beset by yet another crisis, he felt lost and bereft.

As recounted years later in his autobiography, his conversion, as both an artist and a person, came after an anonymous man scolded him: "The talents you have, Mr. Capra, are not your own, not self-acquired. God gave you those talents. They are his gifts to you, to use for his purpose. When you don't use the gifts God bless you with, you are an offense to God and to humanity."

If that sounds like a George Bailey–type revelation, well, that's because Capra's movies unspooled themes and plots close to his Catholic heart. In *Mr. Deeds Goes to Town,* from 1936, Gary Cooper plays a small-town tuba player who outwits his enemies. It's one of Capra's many films that shows the power of goodness to change hearts and prompt conversion, according to film critic Maria Elena de las Carreras Kuntz.

Mr. Smith Goes to Washington, from 1939, similarly depicts an idealistic young senator who overcomes villainous political operatives. In the climactic scene, Stewart, playing the fresh-faced senator, stages a one-man filibuster. Sweating and talking for twenty-four hours, pleading for justice and the American way, he reads from the Constitution, the Declaration of Independence, and the famous "love passage" from Corinthians.

You Can't Take It with You, a 1938 release, is an offbeat comedy about a free-spirited family threatened by a rapacious banker. The film closes with a reconciliation. The movie was a "golden opportunity to dramatize 'Love Thy Neighbor,'" Capra said. "Christ's spiritual law can be the most powerful sustaining force in anyone's life."

Meet John Doe, from 1941, is about a tramp turned into a hero by an ambitious newspaperwoman and used as a pawn by big business. It's a dark movie. Yet the power of faith is asserted. "The meek can inherit the earth when John Does start loving their neighbor," Doe says on a radio show.

Capra could not wear his faith, especially his Catholic faith, on his sleeve in his films; that would have been box-office poison. In any case, art conveys truths and values through story. Meanings are embedded in characters and their choices, circumstances, and crises. It's direction by indirection. Tell the truth, but "tell it slant," Emily Dickinson wrote.

There is a lot to unpack in *It's a Wonderful Life.* People have inherent dignity, even the lowly and humble. Goodness transforms people and communities. Love, a gift freely given, graces our lives through the lives of others. God is present and active in our ordinary lives, and he works through us. George Bailey is an instrument of God, and his desperate prayer is his Gethsemane moment. He finds his way to salvation only when he fully realizes his utter powerlessness.

Capra knew what he was up to. He often said that the Sermon on the

Mount drove his movies. "Movies should be a positive expression that there is hope, love, mercy, justice, and charity," he said in a 1960 interview.

It's a Wonderful Life was a commercial and critical failure when released after the war. Americans were in no mood for an uplifting parable. Capra's masterpiece at last began to get its due in the late 1970s, when it entered the public domain, belonging to no one and, as it turned out, to everyone, as matters of faith do.

The director had summed up his life and art on the final page of his autobiography: "Friend, you are a divine mingle-mangle of guts and stardust. If doors opened for me, they can open for anyone."

Capra died in 1991. He's gone, but he still winks at us, still tells us about God's love, not just in his autobiography but in the very last scene of his beloved Christmas classic. Holding his precious child Zuzu and surrounded by a crowd of loving family and friends, George Bailey looks upward and winks at Clarence. But George is winking at us, too, reminding us that all is well and all will be well.

BIBLIOGRAPHY

Aitken, Tom. "Alfred Hitchcock's Private Passion." *Catholic Digest*, Spring 1999.

Allan, Alfred K. "Big Voice, Big Heart." *Columbia*, July 1966.

Aquilina, Mike. *A History of the Church in 100 Objects*. Notre Dame, Indiana: Ave Maria Press, 2017.

Asay, Paul. "Was Shakespeare Really a Secret Catholic?" *Aleteia*, April 24, 2018.

Auden, W. H. "The Hero Is a Hobbit." *New York Times*, October 31, 1954.

Ball, Ann. "Chocolate." *Catholic Heritage*, January/February 1997.

"Bingo!" *Catholic Digest*, July 1987.

Bjelland, Harley. "The Monastic History of Cheese." *Catholic Digest*, July 1982.

Blake, Richard A., S.J. "Finding God at the Movies ... and Why Catholic Churches Produce Catholic Filmmakers." March 6, 2009.

Boffetti, Jason. "Tolkien's Catholic Imagination." *Crisis*, July 1, 2010.

Borrelli, Christopher. "Sister Act." *Chicago Tribune*, April 23, 2009.

Callahan, Tom. *Johnny U.* Crown Publishers: New York, 2006.

Carr, John Dickson. *The Life of Sir Arthur Conan Doyle*. New York: Harper & Brothers, 1949.

Cloud, Barbara. "The Sister Who Kissed Elvis." *Catholic Digest*, September 1998.

Cobb, Jennifer. *CyberGrace: The Search for God in the Digital World*. New York: Crown, 1988.

Copp, Jay. "Berta Hummel and Her Famous Figurines." *St. Anthony Messenger*, August 1997.

———. "Catholic School Built by a Movie." *St. Anthony Messenger*, March 2001.

———. "God Works Out." *U.S. Catholic*, January 1998.

———. *The Liguori Guide to Catholic USA: A Treasury of Churches, Schools, Monuments, Shrines and Monasteries*. Liguori, MO: Liguori Publications, 1999.

Costello, Damian. "The Catholic Faith of Squanto." *U.S. Catholic*, November 20, 2020.

Creamer, Robert. *Babe: The Legend Comes to Life*. New York: Simon and Schuster, 1974.

Dearborn, Mary. *Ernest Hemingway*. New York: Alfred Knopf, 2017.

Donohue, John W. "Of Many Things." *America*, December 4, 1993.

Feuerherd, Peter. "Marshall McLuhan: Saint of the Internet." *U.S. Catholic*, October 9, 2017.

Fisher, Ian. "This Time, It's the Faithful Hero That Needs the Rescue." *New York Times*, October 29, 2004.

Fishgall, Gary. *Gregory Peck*. New York: Scribner, 2002.

Fitzgerald, Robert, S.J. "Father Ed and AA's Bill." *Catholic Digest*, April 1991.

Flatow, Ira. *They All Laughed … From Light Bulbs to Lasers: The Fascinating Stories behind the Great Inventions That Have Changed Our Lives*. New York: Harper Perennial, 1993.

Foley, Michael. *Why Do Catholics Eat Fish on Fridays? The Catholic Origin to Just About Everything*. New York: Palgrave Macmillan, 2005.

Frawley, Mary Louise. "The Last Days of John Wayne." *Catholic Digest*, May 1981.

Greeley, Andrew. *The Catholic Imagination*. Berkeley: University of California Press, 2000.

_____ . *God in Popular Culture*. Notre Dame, Indiana: Ave Maria Press, 1988.

Greene, Andy. *The Office: The Untold Story of the Greatest Sitcom of the 2000s*. New York: Dutton, 2020.

"Gregor Mendel." *Biography.com*. April 27, 2017.

Hammond, Alexander. "Louis Pasteur: 'The Father of Microbiology' Who Pioneered Vaccine Science." *Foundation for Economic Education*, June 2, 2019.

Hanover, Donna. "The Nun Who Bid Goodbye to Stardom." *Good Housekeeping*, January 1999.

Harbaugh, James, S.J.. "When Ed Met Bill. A Jesuit/AA Connection." *Jesuits Central and Southern*, Fall 2015.

Harrison, Ian. *The Book of Inventions*. Washington, DC : National Geographic Society, 2004.

Hattox, Ralph. *Coffee and Coffeehouses*. Seattle: University of Washington Press, 1985.

Higgins, Earl. *100 Catholic Things to Do Before You Die*. Gretna: Pelican Publishing, 2019.

Holt, Jim. *Why Does the World Exist?* New York: Liveright, 2012.

"I Remember Frank Capra," *Catholic Digest*, January 1992.

Jacquet, Lou. "Remember the Catholic All-Star Team?" *Catholic Digest*, October 1992.

"J. R. R. Tolkien Dead at 81; Wrote 'The Lord of the Rings.' " *New York Times*, September 3, 1973.

Jordan, Meagan. "The Religious Dimensions of Toni Morrison's Literature." *Sojourners*, August 23, 2019.

King, David A. "Hemingway, Catholicism, and His Struggle to Find Meaning." *Georgia Bulletin*, November 17, 2016.

_____ . "McLuhan's Still Current Media Theory 'Deeply Rooted in Catholicism.' " *Georgia Bulletin*, October 24, 2013.

_____ . "The Memorable Legacy of Gregory Peck." *Georgia Bulletin*, March 16, 2016.

King, Thomas M. "The Spirituality of Teilhard de Chardin. A Holy Man and Lover of the World." *America*, March 28, 2005.

Kreisberg, Jennifer Cobb. "A Globe, Clothing Itself with a Brain."

Wired, June 1995.

Krythe, Maymie Richardson. *All about American Holidays*. New York: Harper, 1962.

Kuntz, Maria Elena De Las Carreras. "The Catholic Vision of Frank Capra." *Crisis* 20, no. 2 (February 2002): 38–43.

Lane, Kris. "Five Myths about Christopher Columbus." *Washington Post*, October 8, 2015.

Larson, Robert. "Columbus Sang Salve Regina." *Catholic Digest*, October 1989.

Leaberry, Derek. "Vince Lombardi: How the Catholic Church Formed One of the Greatest Coaches of All Time." *Remnant*, November 7, 2014.

Leach, Michael. *I Like Being Catholic*. New York : Doubleday, 2000.

Levy, Joel. *Really Useful: The Origins of Everyday Things*. Willowdale, Ont.: Firefly Books, 2002.

Longenecker, Dwight. "Ten Signs That Shakespeare Was Catholic." *National Catholic Register*, May 25, 2018.

Luxmoore, Jonathan. "Experts, Historians Explore Shakespeare's Catholic Sympathies." *Catholic News Service*, October 31, 2014.

MacDonnell, Joseph, S.J. "The Jesuit Who Changed the Calendar." *Catholic Digest*, February 1989.

――― . "The Jesuit Who Invented Aviation." *Catholic Digest*, August 1987.

MacRae, Gordon J. "The True Story of Thanksgiving: Squanto, the Pilgrims, and the Pope." *Beyond These Stone Walls* (blog), November 17, 2011.

Maraniss, David. *When Pride Still Mattered: A Life of Vince Lombardi*. New York: Simon and Schuster, 1999.

McCabe, John. *George M. Cohan: The Man Who Invented Broadway*. New York: Doubleday, 1973.

Mendelson, Lee. *A Charlie Brown Christmas*. New York: HarperCollins, 2000.

Meyers, Jeffrey. *Hemingway: A Biography*. New York: Harper & Row, 1985.

Miles, Barry. *Jack Kerouac: King of the Beats*. Croydon, England: Virgon Books, 2010.

———. *Many Years from Now*. New York: Henry Holt, 1997.

Napoli, Lisa. *Ray and Joan*. New York: Dutton, 2016.

Oakes, Kaya. "Holy Words: The Writing of Toni Morrison, Fanny Howe, and Rebecca Brown." *U.S. Catholic*, August 6, 2019.

O'Donnell, Angela Alaimo. "Ernest Hemingway's Dark Night of the Soul." *Church Life Journal*, July 31, 2020.

O'Donnell, Richard. "Casey Never Went to Bat." *Catholic Digest*, April 1988.

Olby, Robert. "Gregor Mendel." *Briticanna.com*. July 20, 1998.

Oosterhoff, Richard. "Faithful Friar or Scientific Sorcerer?" *Christian History*, no. 134, (2020).

Pence, Cain. "Why American Catholics Should Mourn Kobe Bryant's Death." *CatholicPhilly.com*. January 29, 2020.

Perry, Sara. *The Complete Coffee Book*. Vancouver, British Columbia: Raincoast Books, 1991.

Peterik, Jim. *Through the Eye of the Tiger*. Dallas: BenBella Books, 2014.

Phillips, Rod. *A Short History of Wine*. New York: Ecco, 2001.

Polkow, Dennis. "Offbeat: The Ides of March Are Bearing Gifts for Christmas." *Newcity Music*, December 15, 2015.

Remnick, David. *The Bridge: The Life and Rise of Barack Obama*. New York: Alfred Knopf, 2010.

Ripatrazone, Nick. "On the Paradoxes of Toni Morrison's Catholicism." Literary Hub, March 2, 2020.

Ryan, George. "Who Were Daniel Carroll and Thomas FitzSimons?" *Catholic Digest*, September 1987.

San Martin, Inés. "After Maradona's Death, Pope Francis Opens Up and Talks Sports," Angelus News, January 3, 2021.

Seah, Jean Elizabeth. "Louis Pasteur: Father of Microbiology, and a Catholic." Aleteia, November 10, 2017.

Sferrazza, Carl. "Presidents and Papists: A Panorama." *Catholic Digest*, July 1985.

The Slaves of the Immaculate Heart of Mary. "The Catholic Venture of Christopher Columbus." *Catholicism.org*, June 5, 2008.

Solis, Steph. "Copernicus and the Church: What the History Books Don't Say." *Christian Science Monitor*, February 19, 2013.

Spitz, Bob. *The Beatles*. New York: Little, Brown and Company, 2005.

Springsteen, Bruce. *Born to Run*. New York: Simon and Schuster, 2016.

Summer, Anita. "Kate Smith Is Making a Comeback." *Lady's Circle*, October 1975.

Thompson, David. "The Monk Who Discovered Do-Re-Mi." *Catholic Digest*, January 1983.

Thomson, Graeme. *George Harrison: Behind the Locked Door*. Omnibus Press: London, 2015.

Tkacz, Michael. "What Was So Great about Albert?" *Christian History*, no. 134 (2020).

Val Kilmer Newsletter online, March 2001.

Villarrubia, Eleonore. "Casey Jones: Legendary Railroad Engineer and Catholic." *Catholicism.org.*, May 4, 2001.

Weldon, Shawn. "Babe Ruth's Biggest Double." *Catholic Digest*, August 1994.

Wolf, Burton. *What We Eat: The True Story of Why We Put Sugar in Our Coffee and Ketchup on Our Fries*. San Diego: Tehabi Books, 2002.

Wolff, Alexander. "Get on the Stick." *Sports Illustrated*, April 25, 2005.

Woods, Thomas. *How the Catholic Church Built Western Civilization*. Washington, DC: Regnery, 2005.

Young, Mark. "Brother Jasper and the Seventh-Inning Stretch." *Catholic New York*, May 5, 1988.

ACKNOWLEDGMENTS

A book is a group project, not a solo enterprise. The dedicated publishing crew at Our Sunday Visitor expertly transformed my manuscript into a book. They embrace their duties not as a job but as a vocation. I am especially indebted to kindly Senior Acquisitions Editor Mary Beth Giltner, who provided skillful and gracious early guidance, and to eagle-eyed Associate Editor Rebecca Martin, a paragon of clarity and accuracy.

This book is a group project in another way, a case of standing on the shoulders of many writers, historians, journalists, theologians, and others, and restating, reformulating, and repurposing what they saw and recorded. That can be best explained through an analogy.

In high school (a long time ago), I read a piece by columnist Sidney J. Harris of the *Chicago Sun-Times* that has stayed with me all these years. Harris opined that, though we value the entrepreneurial spirit and hail the self-made man, in truth, no one really lifts himself by his bootstraps. He gave as an example a factory CEO. The CEO may be a great leader or thinker, but he cannot be successful without all his skilled workers, who, in turn, were nurtured by teachers and parents.

The list goes on. To succeed, his factory also needs roads, airports, and airplanes; the police; the waste industry; the electrical, gas, and water utilities; indeed, an entire capitalistic marketplace that provides not only an array of stores to sell his product but well-off consumers to buy them. He further needs democratic institutions to ensure that society is safe, fruitful, and productive.

So even the man who "lifts himself by his bootstraps" does not provide his own boots, straps, ladder to climb, or the golden place at the end of the ladder. He relies on others. That's how I was able to write this book. As the bibliography at the end of the text attests, I relied on the research and reasoning of many others to compile these entries. More foundationally, I owe a deep debt of gratitude to my teachers and schools for honing my reading, writing, and thinking skills.

I was no prodigy. It took prodding and patience. In first grade, at the top of a paper, I couldn't even spell my name correctly. My given name is Eugene. Sister Mary Beth at St. Hugh School in Lyons, near Chicago, had fifty restless tykes to guide and command, but she took the time to circle "Eugne" and write a gleeful exclamation mark next to it.

The Sisters of St. Joseph rigorously taught and lovingly shepherded me at St. Hugh, and the Dominican priests at Fenwick High School in Oak Park (hometown of Ernest Hemingway) did the honors for the next four years. My dad, an insurance agent with seven kids born in less than a decade, was able to afford the tuition at Fenwick because of a persuasive intrareligious phone call. Sr. Marlene Schemmel, principal of St. Hugh, beseeched the Dominicans to give me a daily one-hour job to pay for half of my bill. I swept the locker room and shelved books at the school library before or after school, and I applied myself to the challenging curriculum during school hours.

It's only in looking back at my younger self — a lunkhead, like some of my peers — that I fully recognize the dedication and expertise of my teachers. Education is a miracle, an intellectual transubstantiation. You start out unformed and ignorant and end up somewhere on the road to respectability and responsibility.

The greatest lessons were outside the classroom. In the spring of my senior year, I met with my counselor for the last time. Venerable Fr. Bernacki, perhaps because I had sat nearly mute and merely nodding in our sessions for four years, nervous about saying the wrong thing, gave me an emphatic piece of advice. He jabbed my chest with his forefinger and said, "Remember, the Holy Spirit is always inside you." Nearly a half century later, I have not forgotten.

Praise also to my English teachers, a learned and kindly crew, at Knox College in Galesburg, Illinois, and to my journalism professors at Northwestern University. The latter evinced a fierce attachment to getting the facts right. Journalists are no less dogmatic in their beliefs than the priests and nuns who taught me. One of their commandments, a necessary tool for writers of any stripe, was this: "If your mother says she loves you, check it out." Good advice, too.

My saintly mother — may she rest in peace — did love me dearly, and she and my father enjoyed a singularly happy and drama-free fifty-nine-year marriage. The seven of us kids always thanked God we grew up in a stable, loving home. We won the most important lottery, we agreed.

My good fortune continued — providence never so baldly at work — when I went on a retreat for Catholic young adults. On a break, on a long walk in the woods, I prayed fervently to the Blessed Mother to meet a soul mate. That blessed afternoon, I met Laura, a spunky and fun South Side Irish Catholic. We married less than two years later and have shared our lives, each of us giving what we have to the other. She rescued me from myself and centered me in family.

We have been blessed with three sons: Kevin, a Catholic school teacher in the inner city; Andrew, a seminarian; and Brendan, a Notre Dame graduate who works in technology. Foolish younger me: I often fretted about my vocation. Being married and having kids put that angst out to pasture. The glory of God is found not chiefly in the workplace but in home and hearth, where love holds sway. I cannot find the words to express the pleasure and joy of our three sons. Being a parent has been the ultimate experience of my life.

PHOTO CREDITS

Credits listed sequentially by page number.

I. EAT, DRINK, AND BE CATHOLIC

23: Source: National Cancer Institute, photo by Renee Comet.

25: Photo by Pierre Gui on Unsplash.

25: Photo by Linette Simoes via Pixabay.

26: Photo by SKopp. This file is licensed under the Creative Commons Attribution-Share Alike 3.0 Unported license.

28: Hans Braxmeier via Pixabay.

29: Public domain, via Wikimedia Commons

31: Das Gläschen Zur Stärkung, 1880, Eduard von Grützner. Public domain via WikiArt

II. GIANTS OF SCIENCE

37: Photo: Joergens.mi/Wikipedia. This file is licensed under Creative Commons-Share Alike 3.0 Germany

38: Ernest Board, from Wellcome Images, a website operated by Wellcome Trust, a global charitable foundation based in the United Kingdom.

39: Public domain, via Wikimedia Commons

41: Map of the Moon from G. B. Riccioli's 1651 Almagestum Novum. Wikimedia Commons.

44: Amada44, licensed under Creative Commons Attribution-Share Alike 4.0 International license.

46: This file comes from Wellcome Images, a website operated by Wellcome Trust, a global charitable foundation based in the United Kingdom.

48: Pablo Carlos Budassi, licensed under the Creative Commons Attribution-Share Alike 4.0 International.

III. Inventions, Discoveries, and Innovations

53: Saint Elizabeth of Hungary bringing food for the inmates of a hospital. Oil painting by Adam Elsheimer, ca. 1598. Wellcome Collection. Attribution-NonCommercial 4.0 International (CC BY-NC 4.0)

54: Public Domain via WikiArt

56: Manuscript from 1274. Biblioteca Ambrosiana, Milan, Italy. MS D.75 inf, fol. 6r, Wikimedia Commons.

61: Leonello Spada, Public domain, via Wikimedia Commons

63: This file comes from Wellcome Images, a website operated by Wellcome Trust, a global charitable foundation based in the United Kingdom.

65: Public domain via Wikimedia Commons

66: r.a. olea, This file is licensed under the Creative Commons Attribution 2.0 Generic license.

67: This file is licensed under the Creative Commons Attribution-Share Alike 4.0 International license.

IV. Catholic Lingo

71: CDC Public Health Image Library.

71: Public domain, United States Library of Congress's Prints and Photographs division

72: Photo by Marie-Lan Nguyen, licensed under Creative Commons Attribution 3.0 Unported license.

73: Villanova Law Library, licensed under Creative Commons Attribution-Share Alike 2.0 Generic license.

73: Giotto, Descent into Limbo. Public domain, via WikiArt
74: James John Borg, public domain, via Wikimedia Commons
76: Robert Havasy, licensed under Creative Commons Attribution-Share Alike 3.0 Unported license.
77: El Greco, 1607. Public domain via WikiArt

V. America

81: Currier & Ives Print, Library of Congress, Public Domain.
82: Jean Leon Gerome Ferris, Public domain, via Wikimedia Commons
84: Adobe Stock
85: National Portrait Gallery, Smithsonian Institution, Creative Commons Zero License
87: The Miriam and Ira D. Wallach Division of Art, Prints and Photographs: Print Collection, The New York Public Library. Mrs. Thomas M. Randolph, (Martha Jefferson).
88: Public domain, via Wikimedia Commons
90: National Records and Archives Administration, identifier 1192
93: Photograph by Veggies, via Wikimedia Commons
97: Courtesy of the Kate Smith Commemorative Society
99: Photograph by Stephen Becker, Pixabay
101: John M. Chase / Shutterstock.com
103: Photograph by rusticpix_cheryl via Pixabay
104: Photograph by HealthWyze via Pixabay

VI. Holy (Rock 'n' Rollers)

114: Photograph by Takahiro Kyono, licensed under Creative Commons 2.0 Generic license
117: Kevin Scherer, via Flickr
119: Photograph by 54Roberto54, licensed under the Creative Commons Attribution-Share Alike 4.0 International license.
120: Photograph by SolarScott, licensed under Creative Commons Attribution 2.0 Generic license

VII. Writers

125: Photograph by Mikes-photography, Pixabay.

127: Young Ernest Hemingway (back row, fourth from right) at his church in Oak Park, Illinois. Courtesy of Oak Park Library.

131: From Enoch Pratt Library January 29, 1998, © copyright John Mathew Smith 2001. Licensed under the Creative Commons Attribution-Share Alike 2.0 Generic license.

135: Photograph by Alvintrusty, licensed under the Creative Commons Attribution-Share Alike 3.0 Unported license

136: Credit: Portrait of Sir Arthur Conan Doyle, head and shoulders. Wellcome Collection. Attribution 4.0 International (CC BY 4.0)

VIII. Movies and Television

141: Film screenshot, Public domain, via Wikimedia Commons

143: Paramount publicity photographer., Public domain, via Wikimedia Commons

145: Studio, Public domain, via Wikimedia Commons

148: University of Washington Libraries, Special Collections, JSW22897

152: Public domain

154: Foto Anke Meskens, via Wikimedia Commons

160: Pete Souza, Public domain, White House Archives.

161: Photo by David Shankbone, public domain.

162: Photo by Sgt. Michael Connors, public domain.

IX. Sports

172: Photograph by Berthold Werner, public domain.

173: Nan Palmero, licensed under Creative Commons Attribution 2.0 Generic license.

173: Keith Johnston via Pixabay

176: Annette Klinger via Pixabay

180: Public domain, via Wikimedia Commons

182: Sporting News, Public domain, via Wikimedia Commons

182: National Baseball Hall of Fame and Museum.

183: Joel Kaufman, GNU Free Documentation License.

185: LearningLark, licensed under Creative Commons Attribution 2.0 Generic license.

188: John Puslis, Public domain, via Wikimedia Commons

190: Fernando Frazão/Agência Brasil, licensed under Creative Commons Attribution 2.0 Generic license.

191: Oleg Bkhambri (Voltmetro), licensed under Creative Commons Attribution-Share Alike 4.0 International license.

192: Keith Allison, licensed under Creative Commons Attribution 2.0 Generic license.

X. OUTER SPACE TO CYBERSPACE

195: Kanenori via Pixabay

196: Rb85, licensed under Creative Commons Attribution-Share Alike 3.0 Unported license.

197: Johnson Space Center of the United States National Aeronautics and Space Administration, public domain.

198: Johnson Space Center of the United States National Aeronautics and Space Administration, public domain.

200: Johnson Space Center of the United States National Aeronautics and Space Administration, public domain.

203: Screenshot, Twitter.com/pontifex

205:]Bartolome Esteban Murillo, public domain, via Wikimedia Commons

XI. IT'S A CATHOLIC WORLD AFTER ALL

209: Ricardo Helass via Pixabay

211: Unknown; possibly by Pietro Antonio Lorenzoni (1721-1782), Public domain, via Wikimedia Commons

213: Friedrich Haag, licensed under the Creative Commons Attribution-Share Alike 4.0 International license.

216: Cicero Moraes and José Luis Lira.

217: Maryland University Archives, Creative Commons CC) 1.0 Universal Public Domain Dedication.

223: Public domain.

228: Adobe Stock

229: Edwin Torres from USA, licensed under Creative Commons Attribution 2.0 Generic license.

233: Public domain.

ABOUT THE AUTHOR

JAY COPP is the author of *The Liguori Guide to Catholic USA*. He has written hundreds of magazine stories on spirituality and religion, sports, popular culture, history, food and restaurants, current affairs, education, travel, the western suburbs of Chicago, and social justice. He was a reporter for the *New World* newspaper for the Archdiocese of Chicago, an editor at DePaul University, and editor of the *Lion* Magazine (for members of Lions Clubs). One of seven children, he attended Catholic grade school and high school outside Chicago. He and his wife, Laura, are the proud parents of three sons, graduates of Catholic colleges and high school. When not riding his bike, reading, writing, watching high school basketball, or eating chocolate, Jay is sleeping.

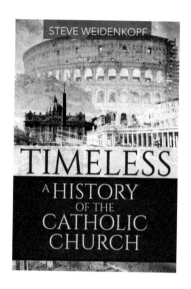

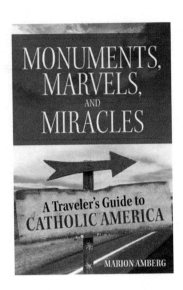

Monuments, Marvels, and Miracles
A Traveler's Guide to Catholic America

Marion Amberg

America's got faith! You'll find it in every state - in grand cathedrals and tiny chapels, in miracle shrines and underwater statues, and even in blessed dirt. Finding these sacred places hasn't been easy - until now! This book takes you to more than 500 of the country's most intriguing holy sites, each with a riveting story to tell.

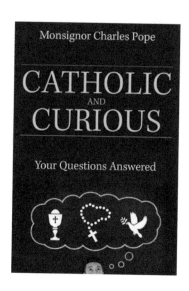